"This book is both a magnificent distillation of many years' work published in five comprehensive volumes and a splendid new work in its own right. Loader's paying attention to and juxtaposing the full range of ancient Jewish and New Testament texts on human sexuality clearly shows the lack of any monochrome view in those texts. His thematic arrangement enables readers to bridge the gap of two millennia with ease and without undue distortion. Most valuable."

— GEORGE J. BROOKE
University of Manchester

"Over the course of the last six years William Loader has engaged in a comprehensive study of sexuality in the literature of Second Temple Judaism and early Christianity. . . . The current volume provides the capstone to this ambitious project, offering a thematically arranged presentation of the evidence of primary sources. In every sense of the word, this is a magisterial contribution to the study of ancient Judaism and early Christianity."

— HAROLD ATTRIDGE
Yale Divinity School

"After publishing eight major monographs devoted to sexuality in antiquity, William Loader has become the international expert best prepared to suggest how each of us can have a healthy sexuality that is faithful to our sacred tradition. This book encompasses areas that are both far-reaching and of great interest to many in contemporary society. Reading it will help us all know more about our vulnerability and how heart is related to genitalia. Loader helps us respect the necessary distance and proximity of the other and how to appreciate a person's otherness and holiness. He writes with insight, skill, and passion. . . . Highly recommended for all who like to read and wish to be better informed."

— JAMES CHARLESWORTH
Princeton Theological Seminary

MAKING SENSE OF SEX

*Attitudes towards Sexuality in
Early Jewish and Christian Literature*

William Loader

WILLIAM B. EERDMANS PUBLISHING COMPANY
GRAND RAPIDS, MICHIGAN / CAMBRIDGE, U.K.

Published 2013 by

Wm. B. Eerdmans Publishing Co.

2140 Oak Industrial Drive N.E., Grand Rapids, Michigan 49505 /

P.O. Box 163, Cambridge CB3 9PU U.K.

Printed in the United States of America

19 18 17 16 15 14 13   7 6 5 4 3 2

Library of Congress Cataloging-in-Publication Data

Loader, William R. G., 1944-

Making sense of sex : attitudes towards sexuality in early Jewish and Christian literature /
William Loader.

pages   cm.   — (Attitudes to sex in early Jewish and Christian literature)

Includes bibliographical references and index.

ISBN 978-0-8028-7095-7 (pbk. : alk. paper)

1. Sex — Biblical teaching. 2. Bible. Old Testament — Criticism, interpretation, etc.
3. Bible. New Testament — Criticism, interpretation, etc. 4. Rabbinical literature —
History and criticism. 5. Christian literature, Early — History and criticism.

I. Title.

BS680.S5L63 2013

261.8'35709015 — dc23

2013022586

Contents

Acknowledgments

This book is the culmination of many years of research and of listening to people as they grapple with what it means to have a healthy sexuality and with how they can best engage with their faith traditions and what they have to say. Sometimes discussions of issues of sexuality have generated hurt and heat, often with very little light. I came to this research because I observed that among the complicating factors in contemporary discussions of sexuality is a lack of reliable information. I therefore sought to fill that gap, both to investigate and report what can be known and to expose what cannot be known or at least what cannot be known with the kind of degree of probability which one hopes for in historical reconstruction. Putting the findings of 5 volumes into one slim account is my attempt to make this information, its conclusions and uncertainties, as widely available as possible.

The research was carried for the most part with the support of an Australian Research Council Professorial Fellowship which I held full time at Murdoch University, Perth, Western Australia, 2005-2010. I am very appreciative of the infrastructure support of the University and of the collegial support of colleagues in Theology there and in the associated Perth Theological Hall of the Uniting Church in Australia, in which I taught for 27 years. The moments of discovery revealed by a proof-reader's pencil continue to amaze me and so, again, I note the great help which Dr Mary J. Marshall has been in that role throughout. Bill Eerdmans has ensured my 5 volumes and 2 others which preceded them saw the public gaze in fine and attractive format.

I also thank Revds Geoff Hurst, Denise Savage, Dr Geoffrey Lilburne, and Professor Amy-Jill Levine, who read and commented on earlier drafts. Finally, my wife of 47 years, Gisela, both read an earlier draft and has had the patience to endure and enjoy seeing me at this task.

William (Bill) Loader, Perth, Easter 2013

Introduction

Sex is not an optional extra. It is part of what and who we are. For some people that is scary, as dealing with all primitive instincts is scary. They fear being overwhelmed and carried away by feelings, as fearful as when they get angry or even overeat or over drink. Indeed for some sex has meant pain and suffering, not because of their own sexuality, but because of what others have done. For other people sex is something they enjoy in themselves and in others. Sexual feeling is as much about the head, or as we more commonly say, the heart, as about the genitalia between our legs. Our attitude towards sex and sexuality is closely related to our attitude towards ourselves and one of our points of vulnerability, which can mean pain or pleasure and tenderness.

But it is not only our personal experience which shapes our attitudes to sex. Our families, communities, including religious communities make a strong contribution and some of their attitudes reach far back over centuries, often preserved in revered texts, such as the Bible. Among these, in turn, there has been controversy, with some wanting to abandon traditional attitudes, some wanting to assert them ever more strongly, and others seeking a path in between. In all such discussions it is paramount to have a clear and well-informed understanding of what ancient writers were saying and, if possible, why, in order to give them the respect and attention they deserve – whatever our response may be to the values they represent.

This book is about listening to what ancient authors were saying. In particular it looks at attitudes to sex in early Judaism and one of the movements it generated, Christianity, in the period from around 300 B. C. E. to around 100 C. E. We cannot recover the experiences of 2000 years ago, let alone enter people's minds or their bedrooms or wherever else they might have expressed their sexuality. We do, however, have a number of writings which reflect attitudes and approaches. In

1

this book "attitudes" refers to how people saw, treated, approached matters relating to sexuality. "Sex" and "sexuality" are used also in a very broad sense of everything which had to do with sex, even if only indirectly, from marriage and divorce, which are about much more than sex, to all kinds of practices which were forbidden or spurned. It deliberately takes a broad view of what might be relevant. It is therefore not a theoretical discussion of the social construction of sexuality or sexualities, though it includes these perspectives when they emerge through the texts.

Behind this book lies extensive and detailed research which I have completed over the last ten years, in particular during five years of holding a full time Australian Research Council Professorial Fellowship at Murdoch University, 2005-2010, to work on the theme. The findings of this research have been published in five volumes, listed in detail at the end of this book. They are: *Enoch, Levi, and Jubilees on Sexuality* (2007); *The Dead Sea Scrolls on Sexuality* (2009); *The Pseudepigrapha on Sexuality* (2011); *Philo, Josephus, and the Testament on Sexuality* (2011) and *The New Testament on Sexuality* (2012). To these one may add three further books and a series of book chapters and articles.[1]

---

[1] *Sexuality and the Jesus Tradition* (Grand Rapids: Eerdmans, 2005); *The Septuagint, Sexuality and the New Testament: Case Studies on the Impact of the LXX in Philo and the New Testament* (Grand Rapids: Eerdmans, 2004); *Sexuality in the New Testament* (London: SPCK; Louisville: Westminster John Knox, 2010); "Proverbs' 'Strange Woman': Image and Reality in LXX Proverbs and Ben Sira, Hebrew and Greek" in *Die Septuaginta – Texte, Theologien, Einflüsse* (ed. Wolfgang Kraus and Martin Karrer; WUNT 252; Tübingen: Mohr Siebeck, 2010) 562-75; "Issues of Sexuality in 1Q28a/1QSa; 4Qpap cryptA Serekh ha-ʿEdah/4Q249d, e," in *Qumran Cave 1 Revisited: Texts from Cave 1 Sixty Years after Their Discovery: Proceedings of the Sixth Meeting of the IOQS in Ljubljana* (ed. Daniel K. Falk; Sarianna Metso; Donald W. Parry and Eibert J. C. Tigchelaar; STDJ 91; Leiden: Brill, 2010) 91-98; "The Strange Woman in Proverbs, LXX Proverbs and *Aseneth*" in *Septuagint and Reception: Essays Prepared for the Association for the Study of the Septuagint in South Africa* (ed. Johann Cook; SVT 127; Leiden: Brill, 2009) 209-23; "The Beginnings of Sexuality in Genesis LXX and Jubilees," in *Die Septuaginta – Texte, Kontexte, Lebenswelten* (ed. Martin Karrer and Wolfgang Kraus; WUNT 219; Tübingen: Mohr Siebeck, 2007) 300-12; "Sexuality and Ptolemy's Greek Bible: Genesis 1-3 In Translation: '... Things Which They Altered For King Ptolemy' (Genesis Rabbah 8.11)" in *Ptolemy II Philadelphus and his World* (ed. Paul McKechnie and Philippe Guillaume; Mnemosyne, Supplements; History and Archaeology of Classical Antiquity, 300; Leiden: Brill, 2008) 207-32; "Sexuality and the Historical Jesus," in *Jesus from Judaism to Christianity: Continuum Approaches to the Historical Jesus* (ed. Tom Holmén; London: T&T Clark, 2007) 34-48; "Jubilees and Sexuality," in *"I Sowed Fruits into Hearts"(Odes Sol. 17:13): Festschrift for Michael Lattke* (ed. Pauline Allen, Majella Franzmann, and Rick Strelan; Early Christian Studies 12; Strathfield: St Pauls, 2007) 117-36; "Sexuality in the Testaments of the Twelve Patriarchs and the New Testament" in *Transcending Boundaries: Contemporary Readings of the New Testament: In Honour of Professor Francis Moloney,*

The purpose of this book is in part to offer a summary of what has emerged from this research in a form that is accessible to the reader who may not have a background education in early Judaism or Christianity. It therefore presents a text in the form of a conclusion, without the discussion of secondary literature which it presupposes and with all references to primary texts of the ancient world not in the text, but in footnotes, to make for easier reading. At the same time, it provides a subject index, not only for this book, but for all five major research volumes, where people can find detailed discussion both of the original texts and of scholarly research related to their themes. In addition it provides an index of ancient sources, though only those cited in this book.

The approach taken in what follows, as in the research on which it is based, has been to listen as far as is possible to what writers were saying in their setting. No researcher endeavouring to do so can escape blind spots and distorting perspectives. The attempt has been made, therefore, to use every tool available to avoid distortion and to elucidate the texts in ways which cohere with the disciplines and methods which have achieved validity among contemporary scholars working in this field. I believe that where people for religious reasons might want to attribute authority to some texts and espouse their views, they will be best served by first hearing what they say. For myself, I sense no obligation, religious or otherwise, to privilege particular ancient texts in a way that shields them from critical investigation. At all times respecting and honouring others, including what they say, entails first and foremost listening to them as far as possible on their terms and not doing so selectively or seeing or hearing only what suits us.

The book's conclusion offers some reflections on the sense both of distance and proximity in relation to these texts and the way people deal with it, including on issues which become highly controversial for communities for whom some of these texts are deemed sacred. The aim is not to resolve such issues, but to enhance awareness of the need for a careful historical perspective as an essential component in addressing them.

While the research has been based on reading these texts in their original language where possible, English translations are used throughout. Texts from the Bible use the New Revised Standard Version, except where I have modified it or provided my own. In this case they are marked with an asterisk. The sources for all other translations are identified within the list of ancient sources. There, too, one finds the abbreviations for each work. Within the main body of this book the first

---

S.D.B. (ed. Rekha M. Chennattu & Mary L. Coloe; Rome: LAS Publications, 2005) 293-309; "Jubilees and Sexual Transgression: Reflections on Enochic and Mosaic Tradition," *Henoch* 31/1 (2009) 48-54; "Attitudes towards Sexuality in Qumran and Related Literature – and the New Testament," *New Testament Studies* 54 (2008) 338-54.

time it refers to one of these works there is a brief description of its date and context.

The main sources for understanding attitudes towards sexuality in the period considered are thus writings, some of them surviving in their original language, some of them only in secondary translations, some in very fragmentary form. Frequently a work not surviving in its original language survives in more than one secondary language. Almost all such works necessarily derive from the more well-to-do or, at least, the better educated. Information about attitudes of most of the population is irrecoverable. Even most of what survives for archaeologists to uncover comes from the buildings of those who could afford lasting materials. On the other hand, especially where texts claim, and apparently are widely deemed, to have authority, including divine authority, we can reckon with the high probability that those listening to them would embrace their attitudes, even if not always following their advice.

This book considers a wide and varied range of literature, which comes to us also from over four centuries and was composed in many different contexts. This, too, must be taken into account. Those centuries saw major change. Already at the beginning of the period there are large settlements of Jews in the east around Babylon and in Egypt around Alexandria. The massive chaos and destruction brought about by Alexander the Great's invasions in the late fourth century probably inspired the horror stories of giants consuming everything and everybody in the earliest parts of the collection known later as *1 Enoch*. It employs the myth of heaven's angels having sex with women to account for both such giants and for the evil spirits which emerged from the corpses of their self-destruction and spread like viruses throughout the world.

The small Judean state endured dominance by Alexander's Greek general Ptolemy and his successors in Egypt during the third century, and, from its end, domination by the successors of another of Alexander's Greek generals, Seleucus, in Syria to the north. Worse still, it had to endure the effects of the wars between the two regimes, which the book of Daniel depicts after, as it puts it, Alexander, depicted as like a billy goat, charged across that world and then crashed, referring to his sudden death in his early thirties.[2] Internal disputes arose in Judea between groups allied to the Ptolemies and the Seleucids, and between those who affirmed and those who hated the Hellenistic fashions they brought. Such disputes divided the community. Apparently harmless tales like that of Tobit, incidentally a rich source of information about weddings, may well serve to legitimise new players, like the Transjordanian Tobiad family.

Finally the Seleucid's desperate fiscal measures, stripping temple wealth, created new chaos in 167 B. C. E. Out of it emerged in 164 B. C. E. the fragile

---

[2] Dan 8:5-8.

beginnings of a Jewish dynasty, the house of Hasmon, under Judas Maccabeus, which made its way by wheeling and dealing among rival Seleucid parties in Syria, where Rome's emergence and demands had put the state into crisis. The new Jewish dynasty gained in strength in proportion to the weakening of its neighbours, rising to great heights by the end of the second century B. C. E. and early first century B. C. E., when its kingdom under John Hyrcanus (134-105 B. C. E) and his son Alexander Janneus (103-76 B. C. E.) matched the extent of Solomon's.

Success and power for the elite priests who thus gained power and merged priesthood with kingship created inevitable disaffections, including among their own. Some of the literature which has survived, especially in the Dead Sea Scrolls, the collection found in the caves on the north west shores of the Dead Sea at Qumran, reflects such disaffected groups, of whom some at this time abandoned the holy city and its temple to promote proper observance elsewhere.

Issues such as relations with foreigners, especially marriage, inevitably arose, both because of the cultural interpenetration which Alexander's world brought and because female captives from Judea's conquests found their way into Jewish households. There was provision in biblical law for the latter to occur,[3] but probably not on the scale that was occurring then. Some saw danger. Society would be infected with idolatry and the forbidden secrets of sorcery which foreign women were feared to possess. The pious separatists engaged in dispute over many issues of observance, including such practices as polygyny, marrying nieces, and sex during menstruation.

Tensions between those resisting marriage to foreigners and those affirming it run through the entire period we consider. Did one look to Ruth and Esther who married foreigners or did one look to Phinehas, who killed a man who brought a foreign woman into his family, Ezra, who outlawed it, dissolving mixed marriages, and Levi and Simeon's massacre of Shechem's people for wanting to affirm his marriage to Jacob's daughter, Dinah? A rewriting of Esther preserved in Greek turns the tale on its head, its heroine now deploring her new estate and with it marriage to any foreigner circumcised or not. Late in our period in the guise of a romance celebrating Joseph's marriage to the Egyptian Aseneth, the author of *Joseph and Aseneth* subtly transforms Levi into her defender, affirming marriage to all who convert.

Loyalists to the hundred year rule of the house of Hasmon, which ended with Pompey's entry into Jerusalem in 63 B. C. E., praised the regime and told the history of its heroes, the Maccabees. The tale of Judith probably served to defend having a woman as ruler, Salome Alexandra (76-67 B. C. E.), widow of Alexander Janneus (103-76 B. C. E.), whom she succeeded. Others looked on with despair

---

[3] Deut 21:10-14.

and like the author of Daniel in the initial crisis inspired hope for change with coded visions, so-called apocalyptic revelations, indicating that change would come soon, bringing God's reign and order. Like Daniel's author, they wrote in the name of heroes of the past, to enhance the authority of their works, such as Jeremiah, Ezekiel, Moses, and even Enoch. They set their ideas of hope in contrast to the sin and corruption of the age, frequently depicted as including sexual wrongdoing.

With regard to the social and political history of the period we are fortunate to have the extensive volumes of Josephus, a priest and general, turned Roman sympathiser after failing to lead the uprising in Galilee against the empire to success during the revolt of 66 – 70 C. E., and who became resident in Rome. He rewrote both the biblical sources and the accounts of later periods in his attempt to convince his Roman audiences and fellow Jews of the great antiquity and integrity of the Jewish faith. His works not only retell history as he saw it, with at times unmistakable bias, but also contain frequent reflections on the behaviour of its main players, including sexual behaviour. His work on Herod alone, in this regard, provides more than enough for a stimulating full length movie.

A forerunner of Josephus, at least in retelling Israel's early history, but written a hundred years earlier, is the *Book of Biblical Antiquities*, sometimes called *Pseudo-Philo*, which selects and supplements the biblical sources, sometimes with surprising observations about sexuality. Going back just over another hundred years is the *Genesis Apocryphon*, which expands the stories of the angels' sex with women and its consequences, and the stories of Abraham and Sarah. Even more significant from that time is the book of *Jubilees*, which not only retells the main stories of Genesis but also appends to them what it claims are instructions given by angels about their importance, much of which applies to sexual matters, with strong disapproval of marriage to foreigners.

We know the actual authors of very few works. Josephus is an exception, as are Paul, at least of seven of his letters, and Philo, who was even known personally to Josephus. Philo and Paul wrote during the early to mid-first century C. E., Josephus, in its later decades. Philo's works form the largest corpus of material to survive. His have little about history, but extensive expositions of the stories and legislation of the first five books of the so-called Old Testament, Genesis, Exodus, Leviticus, Numbers, and Deuteronomy. He, too, was making sense of his faith to his world, but primarily for his fellow educated Jews in Alexandria. He stands at the high point of intellectual development in the large Jewish community at Alexandria in Egypt. Informed by a world view shaped by popular Platonic understandings of the universe and Stoic ethical values, Philo expounds Israel's wisdom as the superior way to right living before God, characterised by control of passions, especially sexual passions, and an ordered life.

Among Philo's predecessors, taking up the best which they saw that Hellenistic culture had to offer and combining it with their own Jewish sense of wisdom and order, were the author of the book of Wisdom, falsely attributed to Solomon; *Pseudo-Phocylides*, framing pithy Jewish instruction as ancient Greek philosophy; *Pseudo-Aristeas*, another framed composition, depicting a symposium where the high priest's delegates impress king Ptolemy 2 Philadelphus of Egypt with their faith's intellectual respectability; and the author, *Aristobulus*, who argued that Plato must have derived his wisdom from Moses.

The development of these intellectual currents in Alexandria was greatly helped by the translation of the Hebrew scriptures of the Jews into Greek, beginning with the first five books, in the first half of the third century B. C. E., as legend has it, under the sponsorship of Ptolemy 2 Philadelphus. Alexandria was not without contact with the Jewish homeland, which also had its tradition of wisdom, proverbially traced back to Solomon. The early second century writer Jesus Ben Sira, another rare instance of our knowing the real author, applied the common sense of his day to life in his world, including extensive reflections on how to deal with sexual relations, good and bad; marriage; daughters; wives; divorce; and women in general, whom he saw as men's nemesis. His grandson then translated his Hebrew into Greek, another forerunner of Philo's exploits. The book of *Instruction*, found at Qumran, tackles similar themes.

The Christian writings from the period consist mainly of the gospels, the first three, Matthew, Mark, and Luke, containing extensive common material, usually and best explained by seeing Mark as the source of the other two, beside a second common source which has not survived, designated "Q". The material relevant to sexual themes is sparse, but enough to suggest that as a Jew Jesus belonged with those who opted for enhanced strictness. Beside that, his was one of the movements of hope looking for radical change, God's reign, but envisaging the world to come as being of a nature where sex would not matter and apparently would not exist. Aside from anecdotes in these gospels and a few in the highly creative drama called the Gospel of John, Paul's letters contain most of the relevant material which warrants attention and is also most misunderstood. Just as Philo's embracing of Hellenistic thought never undermined his belief that God created human beings and so their sexuality cannot be bad in itself, so Paul's embracing of an apparently sexless future utopia never undermined his belief, which agreed with Philo, that sex was part of God's good creation, despite others seeing it quite differently.

The latest works we consider include more writings of an apocalyptic nature, demonstrating that Rome's sack of Jerusalem and its temple in 70 C. E., did not quench people's hopes for change. The Christian book of Revelation, and the Jewish works, *4 Ezra*, the *Apocalypse of Abraham* and *2 Baruch*, keep the hopes alive, but with little reference to matters sexual. This is not the case, however with the *Testaments of the Twelve Patriarchs*, in its present form a second century C. E. Christian publication, but reworking much Jewish material from earlier times. One of its twelve chapters, each devoted to a son of Jacob, makes sexual wrongdoing its main theme and exploits Stoic psychology to reinforce its instructions, but sexual themes inevitably feature also in others, not least concerning Judah and Joseph.

In the chapters of this book which follow the focus is on various areas and aspects, providing a description based on themes. They represent in that sense an abstraction from what has preceded them and is published in the five major volumes, namely, detailed listening to each writing as a whole and its trends and statements. That is where ideas should be tested. As far as possible these contexts have been held in mind as material on common themes had been assembled.

The discussions therefore seek to avoid just producing lists of ideas and instead consistently relate gathered material to its sources and general contexts. That includes, in a broader sense, seeking to understand the material in its imagined social context. The discussions return regularly to that broader social context, in order to remind the reader of its distinctiveness and difference from our own. Ultimately, allowing things to be seen from a proper distance creates clarity and so enables a better basis for engagement and appreciation.

In the Beginning

"In the beginning God created the heavens and the earth."[1] So begins the book of Genesis in the Bible. Its early chapters preserve Israel's reworked version of ancient myths about how the universe came into being. One tells of creation in seven days, with human beings as the climax on day six.[2] One has a reverse order, beginning first with the creation of humankind.[3] By the time of Jesus and his fellow Jewish contemporaries those accounts had long since been read as a single account. We may imagine that most Jews would have shared the basic belief that God created humankind. That means, that in essence, humankind is something good, including all that belongs to being human. Sex is no exception.

In the Beginning according to Genesis 1

Those Jews familiar with the detail could have said a lot more. Their sacred Hebrew text reports that on the sixth day, having created earth and sky, plants and animals during the first five days and declared them all good, God said: "Let us make humankind in our own image".[4] The words, "Let us", may reflect origins of the mythical material in days of belief in more than one God, but in the time we are considering, if these words caused reflection at all, people would have understood them as referring to God and God's angels.

The story goes on to say that God did just that on the sixth day: "So God created humankind in his image. In the image of God he created them. Male and

---

[1] Gen 1:1.
[2] Gen 1:1 – 2:4.
[3] Gen 2:5-25.
[4] Gen 1:26.

9

female he created them."[5] "Humankind" is an appropriate translation for the
Hebrew *adam*, though it can also be used to refer to an individual human being, as
it is in Genesis 2, where it refers to the man, who then bears the name, "Adam".
Here in Genesis 1 it clearly refers to the species, humankind, which it then
identifies as coming in two forms, male and female.

The account then reports God's instructions that they should "be fruitful and
multiply",[6] a command given also to the creatures made on the fifth day,[7] and that
they should rule over all created things. Some speculate that the myth may have
originally intimated that human beings were made male and female because that
is how God is and so they would reflect God's image. As Jews of Jesus' day read
it, the similarity was probably seen in the fact that they were to rule as God rules.

More significantly for our theme, being male and female, engaging in sexual
intercourse to produce offspring, had divine blessing. Following the account of
making other creatures who are to multiply, it would have been automatically
assumed that humankind was also male and female, so mentioning it here gives it
special emphasis. When the account ends with God declaring all that had been
made as "very good",[8] that included human sexuality. Whether with the detailed
account in mind or just with a simple belief in creation, Jews of the time would
not be in any doubt that being human, and that includes being a sexual human
being, male or female, with sexual feelings, was something positive.

In the Beginning according to Genesis 2

Most would also have had some familiarity at least with the gist of what Genesis
2 tells us, and would have read both accounts as one. So while God created
humankind (*adam*) according to Genesis 1, according to Genesis 2 the first human
being (*adam*) was a man. It goes on, then, to tell how God created woman.[9] Most
would have linked the two accounts by seeing the second as explaining the first:
God created human kind, male and female (Genesis 1); and this is how God did it
(Genesis 2).

Behind Genesis 2 is an ancient myth which depicts God as making a model
human being from earth and breathing on it to bring it to life. The account plays
on words in Hebrew. God made the man (*adam*) from the dust of the ground
(*adamah*).[10] Then later it uses a word which means a man, a male human being:

---

[5] Gen 1:27.
[6] Gen 1:28.
[7] Gen 1:22.
[8] Gen 1:31.
[9] Gen 2:18-25.
[10] Gen 2:7.

ish and a word which means woman, a female human being: *ishshah*.[11] The similarity underlines the connection between the two.

In the story of Genesis 2 the sexual theme reappears. God declares that it is not good for the man to be alone: "I will make him a helper as his partner".[12] God then created the animals and brought them to the man to name. But that still left the man without a helper as his partner. It is then that God put the man to sleep, extracted a rib, made a woman out of it, and brought her to the man.[13] He responded: "This at last is bone of my bones and flesh of my flesh; this one shall be called Woman (*ishshah*), for out of Man (*ish*) this one was taken".[14] The account concludes: "Therefore a man leaves his father and his mother and clings to his wife, and they become one flesh".[15]

Becoming one flesh is about union, including sexual union. If the focus in Genesis 1 was on being male and female in order to reproduce, the focus here in Genesis 2 is on companionship and oneness. The ancient myth of woman's creation from man is one of the very early explanations of sexual desire: as the desire to reunite.

In the Beginning according to Aristophanes in Plato's Symposium

Writing in the late fourth century B. C. E. Plato, in his *Symposium*, somewhat tongue-in-cheek, has the comic playwright, Aristophanes, tell a similar story to account for sexual drive. According to Aristophanes human beings once existed in three forms: male (with two sets of male genitalia), female (with two sets of female genitalia) and mixed (with one of each). One day they annoyed the god, Zeus, who in a fit of rage cut them in half from top to bottom. The result of their being cut in half is that ever since the halves have sought their other half: males seeking females; males seeking males; and females seeking females. Aristophanes was making a case for what we call both heterosexual and homosexual sexual union.

This is very different from the account in Genesis, but it shares the notion that something happened in the past to account for sexual desire between partners and it belongs to human nature. The differences are telling: sexual drive in Genesis is not a punishment but an element of God's creation, something positive. Similarly, Genesis does not contemplate categories beyond simply male and female, and this remains a constant feature in Jewish thought of the time, so that anything other than that, such as homosexual desire, is seen as deliberately perverse.

---

[11] Gen 2:23.

[12] Gen 2:18.

[13] Gen 2:21-22.

[14] Gen 2:23.

[15] Gen 2:24.

Sexual Union and Social Reality

Returning to the account in Genesis, it depicts the re-union of male and female not only as meeting God's concern about the man being alone, but also as the foundation for a social reality. The two become one flesh because the man "clings to his wife".[16] The word, "clings to" also means "sticks to". Becoming one flesh refers not to a single moment of ecstasy, such as may occur in a single act of sexual intercourse, but to an ongoing state.

That a man "leaves his father and mother" indicates a new social reality, the beginning of a new household. As we shall see in the next chapter, the normal pattern was for a woman to leave her household for the man's, but it was also true that the man had to establish his own household and in that sense leave behind his parents as well, though in a different sense. The Genesis story became the basis for reflection on marriage. Marriage was seen as the context where sexual intimacy had its proper place.

Change for the Worse

Immediately following these words about becoming one flesh, we read that the man and woman were naked and not ashamed.[17] That then changes after the woman and then the man disobey the instruction not to eat of the tree of life in the mythical garden of Eden and follow the snake's advice to do so. Here we have another ancient story. It is designed in part to explain why genitalia should be covered by clothes. It could have implications for how sexuality was seen, for instance, as something to be ashamed of and as bad, but that does not seem to be the intent. Instead, the focus is human disobedience and its consequences.

According to the story those consequences include being banished from the garden, but they do pertain also to human sexuality, at least as far as the woman is concerned. God declares to the woman: "I will greatly increase your pangs in childbearing; in pain you shall bring forth children, yet your desire shall be for your husband, and he shall rule over you".[18] Again we are dealing with a story explaining why things are the way they are, as myths do: why childbirth is painful. It also makes direct mention of desire, here, sexual desire. While it could be read as giving the woman sexual desire as if it were something she did not have before, it was more likely understood as meaning that woman's sexual desire (which she naturally has by virtue of creation from the man, and which he has for the same reason) will keep leading to her becoming pregnant and suffering the

---

[16] Gen 2:24.
[17] Gen 2:25.
[18] Gen 3:16.

pain of childbirth again and again. Her subordination to him ("he shall rule over you")[19] appears to be a consequence of her changed state of vulnerability. Whether the myth assumes that before this they were equal partners is not clear, but seems unlikely, or, at least, this was not how those who retold the stories read them.

Retelling the Creation Story in the Book of Jubilees

We can understand why Jews of the period, brought up on these kinds of stories or at least on the fundamental belief in creation which underlies them, had a basically positive attitude towards sexuality as something which belonged to being human and had its proper place in marriage and household. Beyond imagining, we also have evidence from writings of the time that this was so.

One remarkable instance of retelling the Genesis stories is to be found in the writing called *Jubilees*. It was written somewhere around the early to mid second century B. C. E. Copies of the full text have survived in translation in Ge'ez, the language of the Ethiopian church, but much older fragments of the original Hebrew version have been found among the scrolls found by the Dead Sea, dating back to the late second century B. C. E.

Its author merges the two accounts in Genesis 1 and 2. He notes that God created humankind, one man and a woman, on the sixth day, and that their task was to rule all, but makes no mention of their being in God's image or the command to reproduce.[20] He also omits formation from the dust of the ground and God's concern about the man being alone, but later goes on to report that on the sixth day of the second week God had the angels bring all the animals to Adam over five successive days.[21]

The author then adds: "Adam was looking at all of these – male and female among every kind that was on the earth. But he himself was alone; there was no one whom he found for himself who would be for him a helper who is like him".[22] Already Adam senses the desire for such union, including sexual union. He wants a partner, too. It is then that the author has God reiterate that concern, picking up from Genesis God's view that it was not good for the man to be alone.[23] In Genesis God had raised that issue before the creation of the animals. Here the issue relates directly and only to Adam's desire for a partner.

Jubilees then brings the account of God putting Adam to sleep, taking the rib, making the woman, but instead of bringing her to him, as in Genesis, God brings

---

[19] Gen 3:16.

[20] *Jub.* 2:14.

[21] *Jub.* 3:1.

[22] *Jub.* 3:3.

[23] *Jub.* 3:4; cf. Gen 2:18.

Adam to her.[24] At least that is what appears to be the best reading among the manuscripts. It then adds: "and he knew her",[25] which thus forms the climax of the story. The knowing may simply have meant recognition, but more probably reflects the use of "know" to mean engage in sexual intercourse. The author may have been thinking ahead to what immediately follows, where the Genesis text speaks of their becoming one flesh.[26] Here, as it seems, sexual union is the focus of both Adam's desire and God's intent. The overall effect of the retelling is to make sexual union between man and woman something very positive and special.

The historian Josephus, writing his *Antiquities of the Jews* (*A.J.*) in Greek in the late first century C. E., appears to stand under the influence of *Jubilees* in his retelling of Genesis 1 – 3. He strips the account of the creation of humankind on the sixth day to a bare minimum. Having mentioned that God made the animals male and female, he simply adds: "on this day also he formed humankind".[27] That is it. Gone is any reference to "Let us make", to God's image, to ruling creation, and to being fruitful and multiplying.

We find echoes of *Jubilees* in his account of the animals: "God brought before Adam the living creatures after their kinds, exhibiting both male and female".[28] God then named them, unlike in Genesis where Adam did so, and as in *Jubilees* they were not potential partners. Rather God saw "Adam to be without female partner and consort [lit. not having sexual relations/intercourse with a female] (for indeed there was none)" and observed him "looking with astonishment at the other creatures who had their mates".[29] So here, too, the focus is on sexual companionship such as Adam had seen among the animals.

Josephus then briefly reports God's response in Gen 2:20-23 in creating woman, making no mention of Adam's response nor of Gen 2:24 about becoming one flesh. As in *Jubilees*, he has them only now brought into the garden, but it is not a sanctuary as there.[30] Gone is any reference to nakedness. Later when it appears, it is unrelated to sexuality.[31] God's judgement falls first on Adam for "yielding to a woman's counsel" (i.e. inferior counsel in Josephus' view).[32] That is deemed even more serious than the sin, itself. The judgement on the woman relates to pain in childbirth but otherwise Josephus makes no mention of "desire" or returning to her husband, so leaves sexual desire untouched by any negative

---

[24] *Jub.* 3:4.

[25] *Jub.* 3:5.

[26] Gen 2:24.

[27] *A.J.* 1.32.

[28] *A.J.* 1.35.

[29] *A.J.* 1.35.

[30] *Jub.* 3:12.

[31] *A.J.* 1.44.

[32] *A.J.* 1.49.

connotation. He also omits her being ruled by him, since that, for Josephus, is implied already in her being created an inferior being.

Becoming one flesh

Among the scrolls found at the Dead Sea were a number of writings which appear to have been part of a collection. They included all of what is commonly called the Old Testament (except the book of Esther), but also a number of other Jewish writings, some previously known, like *Jubilees*, others, previously unknown. One of these is the book of *Instruction*, which presents advice and instruction on how to live. It was written in Hebrew, probably early in the second century B. C. E. It includes instruction about marriage, but is very fragmentary, so that its content must be reconstructed by collating its multiple copies.

It is very unusual in including instruction given directly to women, urging them to honour their husbands, though the lines are poorly preserved.[33] Instructions to husbands are more extensive. They refer more than once to "his womb", the assumption being that, having become one flesh, hers is his.[34] We find allusions to his rule over her, to woman's origin from man and therefore the need to hold her in honour, and to her being the helper of his flesh, associated with becoming one flesh.[35] In other words it reflects an exposition of the Genesis stories in relation to marriage in a way that strongly affirms marriage and sexuality within it. It clearly sees the man as the head of the partnership, typical of society at the time.

The book of *Tobit*, composed in Aramaic also in the early second century B. C. E., tells the tale of Tobit's son, Tobias, who travels abroad on his father's instructions to find and marry a certain Sarah from his extended family. On the wedding night Tobias' prayer echoes the Genesis account: "You made Adam, and for him you made his wife Eve as a helper and support. From the two of them the human race has sprung. You said, 'It is not good that the man should be alone; let us make a helper for him like himself'."[36] He continues: "I am now taking this sister of mine, not because of sexual immorality but in truth/legitimately"*.[37] The issue is not sexual desire, as if he is claiming he has none, as some have read it. The point he is making is that she is an appropriate partner for him and he is not therefore engaging in sexual promiscuity or exploitation.[38]

---

[33] 4QInstr³/4Q415 2 ii.

[34] 4QInstr³/4Q415 9 2; 4QInstr⁸/4Q423 3a.

[35] 4QInstr^b/4Q416 2 iii.19-21; 4QInstr^e/4Q418a 16b+17 3.

[36] Tobit 8:6.

[37] Tobit 8:7.

[38] Cf. Tobit 4:12.

Another tale playfully alludes to the Genesis stories. It is found in 1 Esdras 3:1 – 5:6, in a work revising Ezra and Nehemiah, and composed originally in Aramaic sometime in the second century B. C. E. This tale depicts a competition among Darius' bodyguards to see who can make the best argument for what is most powerful in the world. In the fun that follows, one argues for wine, another for the king, another for women, and the fourth for truth, which finally wins the contest. The case for women[39] depicts men as dependent on women from birth onwards, captivated by attractive women to the point of irrationality, and so abandoning all else that they value in order to please them. It then uses the Genesis text about becoming one flesh[40] to declare that a man leaves his own father who brought him up, and his own country, and clings to his wife; and ends his days with his wife, with no thought for his father or his mother or his country. Citing acts of bravery on behalf of women, it again alludes to the same Genesis text in declaring: "A man loves his wife more than his father or mother".[41] Beyond the humour we see what is clearly a norm derived from the Genesis texts: permanent joining in an ongoing and loving relationship.

Becoming One Flesh in Jesus and Paul

Against the background of such texts it is then not surprising to read an anecdote about Jesus in which he makes the point of the permanence of marriage using the same texts. Confronted by the issue of divorce Jesus asserts: "From the beginning of creation, 'God made them male and female'.[42] 'For this reason a man shall leave his father and mother and be joined to his wife, and the two shall become one flesh'.[43] So they are no longer two, but one flesh".[44] He cements the sense of permanence with the words: "Therefore what God has joined together, let no human being separate"*.[45] We shall consider its implications for Jesus' attitude towards divorce in the next chapter, but for the present it is unambiguous in its affirmation of the union (including sexual union) of man and woman in marriage. Its focus is not utilitarian: as if he were to say, becoming one flesh is only legitimate if it is for the sake of bringing children into the world. Rather it emphasises the union and its permanence.

Paul argues similarly, using the same Genesis text about becoming one flesh, though he applies it in a quite different direction. He uses it to warn the

---

[39] 1 Esd 4:13-32.

[40] 1 Esd 4:20; cf. Gen 2:24.

[41] 1 Esd 4:25; cf. Gen 2:24.

[42] Gen 1:27.

[43] Gen 2:24.

[44] Mark 10:6-8.

[45] Mark 10:9.

Corinthians against sexual intercourse with an illicit sexual partner, usually taken to be a prostitute. "Do you not know that whoever is united to a prostitute becomes one body with her? For it is said, 'The two shall be one flesh'."[46] According to Paul, sexual intercourse creates a new permanent relationship of oneness and by implication severs all previous such relationships, which is why he deems anyone doing so as having cut themselves off from Christ.

In Paul's communities we find the metaphor of becoming one flesh developed further, when in Ephesians the author likens the relationship between the church and Christ to a marriage, where Christ is the husband and the church, the bride. It is a daring metaphor, which we can see that the author senses when he designates it as a "great mystery".[47] Philo, the Jewish philosopher who lived in Alexandria, Egypt, in the first half of the first century C. E. and produced an extensive body of writings, does something quite similar when depicting the relationship between God and humankind in whom God sows the seed of immortality and the virtues. He, too, calls it a "mystery".[48]

Both Paul and Philo are primarily using the Greek translation of the Old Testament, the Septuagint. Before we turn further to Paul and Philo, it is important to note the spectrum of meanings opened up in the Greek version of the creation stories, which largely overlaps with, but at times goes beyond that of the Hebrew.

The Creation Stories in Greek

The translation of Genesis into Greek took place in Egypt, almost certainly during the reign of Ptolemy 2 Philadelphus, 283-246 B. C. E. Making humankind in God's image could evoke for some Greek readers, familiar with Plato, a range of new possible meanings. They would include seeing Gen 1:27 about making humankind male and female as a reference to the making of an archetype or in Platonic terms the "idea" of humankind. Then one could see Genesis 2 as describing the actual creation of the "real" human beings on the basis of that model.

It must have been complicated for the translators dealing with the word, *adam*. Greek also had a word, *anthropos*, which could mean a human being, like *adam*, but by the time they reached Gen 2:16 they decided that *adam* there should be translated as a name, Adam. Greek speakers using Genesis could easily see also the references to *anthropos* as primarily to a male.

---

[46] 1 Cor 6:16; cf. Gen 2:24.

[47] Eph 5:32.

[48] *Cher.* 48-49.

It was even more difficult to reproduce the Hebrew play on words, when it referred to humankind (*adam*) being made from the dust of the "ground" (*adamah*), the "earthling".[49] Instead it simply states that the man, *anthropos*, was made from the dust of the earth, *ge*, so the connectedness of humankind to earth, earthling, was lost. Similarly, it was impossible to reproduce the play on words in the creation of "woman" (*ishshah*) from "man/male" (*ish*), possible still in English ("*male-female*").[50] The connection implied in the words is lost. Instead it has Gen 2:23 declare: "She shall be called woman/wife (*gyne*), for she was taken from her man/husband (*aner*)". Adding "her" shifts the focus to marriage.

Intentionally or not, the effects of some parts of the translation can easily result in people thinking of a hierarchy. Thus the translators produce in Gen 2:18 an echo of Gen 1:26. In the original Hebrew in 1:26 God says, "Let us make" and in 2:18, "I shall make". The Greek has "Let us make" in both instances, so that 2:18 recalls 1:26. In addition whereas in the Hebrew in both Gen 2:18 and 2:20 God speaks of making "a helper as his partner", the translators change 2:20 so that it reads: "a helper like him". This again recalls Gen 1:26 where God created the man in God's likeness. As a result a reading can emerge according to which, as man is in the image and likeness of God, so woman is in the image and likeness of man. It need not be read that way, but it is clear that some saw it that way, including Paul, who uses it to urge that women remain in their place because "Christ is the head of every man, and the husband is the head of his wife, and God is the head of Christ"[51] and man "is the image and reflection of God; but woman is the reflection of man".[52] "Helper" which need not imply subordination in either Hebrew or Greek, then takes on a sense of inferiority, given the hierarchy in the context.

In Gen 2:24 which describes a man as leaving his mother and father and clinging to his wife to become one flesh, the Greek word used for cling or stick or join can imply that someone else is involved: "and be joined" by someone. In the anecdote told about Jesus, his final words, "What God has joined together, let no one separate",[53] may be picking up this possibility.

As the Greek translation moves into Genesis 3, it produces some more ambiguity. Confronted by God about her deed, Eve declares that the snake tricked her.[54] Unlike the Hebrew word, the word used in Greek for tricked can also mean seduced. Inevitably some would read it that way, importing sexual connotations into Eve's sin, as we shall see shortly.

---

[49] Gen 2:7.
[50] Gen 2:23.
[51] 1 Cor 11:3.
[52] 1 Cor 11:6.
[53] Mark 10:9.
[54] Gen 3:13.

Then in depicting God's words of judgement addressed to the woman,[55] the Greek translated the Hebrew word for "desire" *teshukah* with the word *apostrophe* which can mean either "return" or "refuge". So what began as, "Your desire shall be for your husband" becomes "your return shall be to your husband" or "your refuge shall be with your husband". The change may well be because the Hebrew word had come to be associated in meaning with a similar sounding word, *teshubah*, which did in fact mean return. Removing the word meaning, desire, could thereby eliminate the sexual reference, especially if the Greek word is read as "refuge". If, however, the translators had in mind that the judgement was that the woman would keep returning to her husband and becoming pregnant, or if subsequent readers read it this way, the sexual aspect is retained. It would be implied in the woman constantly returning to her husband and becoming pregnant again.

The translators may have sensed a parallel with what was said to the man. For there, too, the translators use the same word "return" *apostrepho* to describe the man's return to "the earth", from which according to the Greek translation of Gen 2:7 he was taken.[56] The effect is to create a reading according to which the outcome of human sin is that the man must return to his origins: earth; and the woman must return to hers: the man. These are possibilities and not the only ones. They raise all kinds of options for interpreting the creation stories among those using the Greek translation.

Interpreting the Greek Text

We have already noted how Paul assumes the hierarchy between women, men, Christ, and God, which the Greek translation makes possible. He also exploits the wider meaning of the word *exapatao*, which it has Eve use in response to God's accusation, namely "seduce". So Paul writes to the Corinthians that he does not want them to be "seduced" (*exepatesen*) by false teachers in the way that Eve was seduced by the snake, but wants to present them to Christ as a chaste virgin.[57] Paul's sense of order derived both from his understanding of Genesis and his sense of what was good order or according to nature in his society, as we shall see in the next chapter.

The author of 4 Maccabees, writing in the late first century C. E. has the mother of the seven sons martyred for their faith by the Seleucid king. It also uses the Greek version of Genesis and the idea of seduction. Thus she declares: "I was a pure virgin and did not go outside my father's house; but I guarded the rib from

---

[55] Gen 3:16.

[56] Gen 3:19.

[57] 2 Cor 11:2-3.

which woman was made. No seducer corrupted me on a desert plain, nor did the destroyer, the deceitful serpent, defile the purity of my virginity".[58]

Some decades after Paul's time we see a similar combination of accepting what were seen as the best of social norms and an appeal to Genesis in the letter to 1 Timothy, which was composed in Paul's name and so appealed to his authority. The author reinforces what already Paul saw as appropriate behaviour for most women, that is, that they not engage in public discourse in gatherings for worship, but remain silent, keeping their questions for later when they can learn from their husbands.[59] Paul's letters show that he admitted exceptions, typical of Jews of his time, but his imitator rules out exceptions, declaring that no woman may teach or have authority over a man (which for him teaching would imply). He then reinforces this ruling with an appeal to Genesis: "For Adam was formed first, then Eve; and Adam was not deceived, but the woman was deceived and became a transgressor. Yet she will be saved through childbearing, provided they remain in faith and love and holiness, with modesty."[60]

The argument that man was prior and so superior reflected a widespread assumption about first being prior, older being better. The blaming of Eve as the first to sin was not new. Others had employed it,[61] though by contrast the author of 4 Ezra, struggling to make sense of evil in the decades after the catastrophe of the destruction of the Jewish temple by the Romans in 70 C. E., makes no reference to Eve at all in referring to the first sin.[62] The claim that Adam was not deceived probably means: was not the first to be deceived, because the author would hardly deny that he then went along with Eve, but it certainly asserts Adam's superiority.

The explanation that "she will be saved through childbearing" has generated a range of explanations, mainly in an attempt to make sense of "saved" as in some way referring to her spiritual salvation, not least because the Greek word is frequently used with this sense. It makes much clearer sense, however, to see here not a reference to salvation, but an allusion to Gen 3:16, the sequel to the sin. Her salvation in that sense, her security, is that she will keep returning to her husband. Her refuge will be in belonging to a marriage and submitting to her husband. That is the best and safest way for women to live according to the author.

The most extensive interpretations of Greek Genesis are to be found in the voluminous writings of Philo. According to Philo, who was well versed in Platonic philosophy, God created the ideas or patterns for all things at the

---

[58] 4 Macc 18:7-8.

[59] 1 Cor 14:34-35; 1 Tim 2:11-14.

[60] 1 Tim 2:13-15.

[61] Sir 25:24 (possibly); *2 Enoch* 30:17; 31:6; *Sib. Or.* 1:42-45; and *Apoc. Mos.* 7:2; 10:2; 32:2; and 29:9.

[62] 4 Ezra 3:4-7; similarly *2 Baruch* 56:5.

beginning of the first day of creation, and on the other days made the categories or species for each genus, including the genus, human being. The matter is complicated because Philo expresses himself differently in different texts. With regard to the Genesis texts there is a consistency, however, in the affirmation that it was God who created humankind at all levels, including the man moulded from clay. This is so even though he takes the words, "Let us make" as indicating that God had helpers and that it is their fault that human beings have a propensity to go wrong.[63] This is still a long way from Plato who suggested that God made only the soul and that lesser beings made the body, which traps it in chaos.[64] Philo is, after all, a Jew and so cannot deny God's creation. For all its potential for evil the human constitution is not evil in itself, according to Philo. That includes its passions and not least sexual desire and the pleasure associated with it.

In his account of the creation of woman[65] Philo cannot help himself in portraying woman as trouble, but then also cannot deny God's hand in the creation. In his elaboration of Gen 2:24 about becoming one flesh, Philo even finds a place for sexual pleasure. It makes the intercourse work, he argues, and so enables human reproduction to occur. It is in that context something positive. He uses the language of two halves coming together, reminiscent of Aristophanes' myth in Plato, referred to above, but as something positive, willed by God.

Much that we read in Philo seems excessively negative about the human body, its passions, including its sexuality, and women as a lower form of being driven by passions, but Philo remains loyal to the Genesis accounts in not surrendering to a dualism or denigration of creation in itself. Rightly ruled and ordered, creation is good. That includes sexual relations. Indeed they become a model for Philo's expositions of how different aspects of reality should relate: God and the earth; God and people (the great "mystery");[66] the mind and virtue; the mind and the senses. Not a wicked and evil act, sexual intercourse is a model for right relationships when properly directed.

In interpreting God's judgement on the woman and the man in Gen 3:16-19 Philo does not generalise. At times he depicts the sentence of death, which he takes as spiritual death, as applying only to foolish men.[67] On women, Philo adds to the pain of childbirth, the pain of bringing up children.[68] Women's inferiority, including their domination by passions, including sexual passion, stems not from the judgement expressed in Gen 3:16, but from their creation. Even then he

---

[63] *Opif.* 72-75.
[64] *Tim.* 42E 5-6.
[65] *Opif.* 151-152.
[66] *Cher.* 48-49.
[67] *Leg.* 3.251.
[68] *Opif.* 167.

expresses the opinion that they are less interested in sex than men, who are nevertheless better equipped to rein in the horses of their desire.[69]

If Philo barely holds onto Genesis amid his warnings against the dangers of the human embodiment and of women as its most blatant expression, others were prepared to let the positive go, and declare sexual passion evil.

The *Sibylline Oracles*, is a collection of oracles composed in Greek in imitation of oracles of the ancient Erithrean prophetess, called a sibyl, as a vehicle for Jewish teaching and prophecy. Its earliest sections, found in Book 3, were composed in the second century B. C. E. in Egypt. Books 1 and 2, composed as a single work, probably in the second half of the first century C. E., and expanded by a Christian interpolator in the second century, give a very different account of the garden of Eden. They report that God created a beautiful young man, using his own image as a pattern, and placed him in a garden of paradise. "But he being alone in the luxurious plantation of the garden desired conversation and prayed to behold another form like his own."[70] The account then reworks Gen 2:20-23, the creation of woman, to the effect that the young man was "amazed in spirit, rejoicing, such a corresponding copy did he see".[71] Accordingly "they conversed with wise words, which flowed spontaneously … They neither covered their minds with licentiousness nor felt shame, but were far removed from an evil heart; and they walked like wild beasts with uncovered limbs".[72] All sexual references have gone. The man's interest is conversation not sex. The account mentions the sin, which is not sexual, but nothing is said of the judgement on the woman and the man. On the contrary they are sent out into the earth which is not cursed and only then are instructed to be fruitful and multiply. Apparently human mortality, the result of sin, is what makes propagation necessary and so justifies sexual desire,[73] a view shared also by the author of *2 Baruch*, which, like *4 Ezra*, was written in the aftermath of the destruction of the temple in 70 C. E. Thus the author writes of the passion of parents, their "bubbling up", as an unavoidable necessity after humans became mortal.[74] They need it for reproduction of the species. Its vision of hope still has a place for at least moderate passion and the bearing of children, which it promises will then be painless.[75]

Much more radical is the *Apocalypse of Moses*, one of a number of related works which retell the story of Adam and Eve, but the earliest extant work, written possibly in the late first century or early second century C. E. The snake

---

[69] *QG* 3.47.

[70] *Sib. Or.* 1:26-28.

[71] *Sib. Or.* 1:32-33.

[72] *Sib. Or.* 1:33-37.

[73] *Sib. Or.* 1:57-58.

[74] *2 Baruch* 56:6.

[75] *2 Baruch* 73:7.

gives Eve the forbidden fruit only after it has sprinkled poison on it, identified as desire, understood as sexual desire.[76] In response to God's judgement Eve declares that she will "never return to the sin of the flesh", meaning sexual intercourse, which God then promptly contradicts in the words of Gen 3:16, "because of the enmity which the enemy has placed on you, you will return to your husband, and he will rule over you".[77] We see here the echo of the Greek translation in the reference to the "return" to her husband. Sexual desire is sin. At most, sexual intercourse may be warranted for propagation of the species, but sexual passion is here something from the devil. Behind this reconstruction may well lie the reading of Eve's reply to God in Gen 3:13 as indicating that the snake seduced her in some sense.

The Myth of the Watchers and the Beginning of Evil

The sin of Adam and Eve is not the only explanation for what went wrong with the world in the beginning. Genesis provides a brief account of another explanation,[78] but one extensively elaborated and attested elsewhere. It tells of angels who misbehaved. The Genesis story simply reports that as the human population increased on earth and daughters were born, "the sons of God saw that they were fair; and they took wives for themselves of all that they chose".[79] Two verses later we read: "The Nephilim (giants) were on the earth in those days—and also afterwards—when the sons of God went in to the daughters of humans, who bore children to them. These were the heroes that were of old, warriors of renown".[80] The context speaks of human wickedness and goes on to tell of Noah and the flood as an act of judgement on humankind. The passage makes no direct connection between what the "sons of God" did and human wickedness, though we may suspect that many Jews would have linked them and seen the action of the "sons of God" (angels) as a breach of proper order. Otherwise it simply explains how the great heroes of the past came into being.

As in Genesis 1 – 3 we are dealing with traces of an ancient myth. It comes to us in fuller form in *1 Enoch*, another work, like *Jubilees*, preserved in Ge'ez translation by the Ethiopian church, but of which fragments of the original Aramaic version have been found among the scrolls discovered at the Dead Sea. It is, in fact, a composite work, consisting of five major parts. The first and oldest is *1 Enoch* 1 – 36, known as the *Book of the Watchers*, and dating back to as early as the fourth century B. C. E. Its story already reflects the joining together of earlier

---

[76] *Apoc. Mos.* 19:3.

[77] *Apoc. Mos.* 25:3-4.

[78] Gen 6:1-3.

[79] Gen 6:2.

[80] Gen 6:4.

diverse material. At the heart of the myth is an act of sexual intercourse between the Watchers and women.

In the biblical account "sons of God" was a way of referring to angels. "Watchers" also refers to angels. The account at the core of the *Book of the Watchers* is a retelling of the story. In its earliest form in *1 Enoch* 6 – 11 it describes how the angels found human women very attractive and, after quelling their qualms, resolved to go down and have sex with the women and produce children.[81] The account names their leader as Shemihazah and their number as 200.

It then reports what happened as a result,[82] describing their intercourse as an act in which the holy angels defiled themselves. They also taught the women magic, secret charms, and plant medicine. The women became pregnant and gave birth to giants, whom it calls Nephilim (as in Gen 6:4). These giants ate up all the food meant for human beings and then started eating people, and finally set to killing and eating each other and drinking blood, an act abhorrent among Jews. This unmitigated disaster was further complicated by an angel called Asael, who taught people metallurgy, so that they could make weapons of war, but also bracelets and ornaments.[83] The story of Asael may well have once existed separately. He taught people how to engage in war and taught women how to make cosmetics for their adornment, which made them all the more alluring to their guests. Women were now not just victims of the Watchers' passion, but also complicit in their deeds.

The angels, Michael, Sariel, Raphael, and Gabriel, saw what was happening, heard the cries of humankind, and sought divine intervention.[84] Accordingly God sent Sariel to prepare Noah for the flood, sent Raphael to capture and bind Asael, had Gabriel destroy the "bastards", as it described the offspring, by setting them at war with each other, and told Michael to capture the rest and tie them up until judgement day.[85] God then promised a brighter future for the righteous with abundant resources and large families: "They will live until they beget thousands, and all the days of their youth and their old age will be completed in peace".[86] "Every vine that will be planted on it will yield a thousand jugs of wine, and of every seed that is sown on it, each measure will yield a thousand measures".[87]

So permanent disaster was averted and replaced by a vision of goodness and abundance. While not directly addressed, that vision implies a positive stance

---

[81] *1 Enoch* 6:1-8.

[82] *1 Enoch* 7:1-6.

[83] *1 Enoch* 8:1-4.

[84] *1 Enoch* 9:1-11.

[85] *1 Enoch* 10:1-15.

[86] *1 Enoch* 10:17.

[87] *1 Enoch* 10:19.

towards sexual engagement, not least to produce appropriate offspring, and overall a reaffirmation of creation as good when not distorted and twisted by acts of perversion. The preceding chapters, *1 Enoch* 1 – 5, had emphasised the importance of keeping to the way God had ordered creation, which is precisely what the Watchers failed to do.

While disaster was averted, as the giants self-destructed, danger was not. Those women and men kept their newly learned secrets. Alas, weapons of war would be made; women would harbour what was seen as dangerous and forbidden knowledge and would continue to adorn themselves seductively. So at one level the story serves to explain why things can still go wrong. If, as is likely, it was written at the time that the armies of Alexander the Great and his successors ravaged the land, one can understand that it could give some comfort to know why such disaster can occur.

The act of intercourse between angels and women would have been as abhorrent to Jews as an act of intercourse between a human and an animal. This has caused many to wonder whether the story is also targeting other specific kinds of sexual wrongdoing in some way. Foreign women had a reputation for practicing witchcraft and magic. So the story may be an implied warning against marriage to foreigners, a common concern among Jews of this period. Angels served as priests in the heavenly temple, so perhaps priests on earth were the intended target. Had some of them entered forbidden marriages with outsiders? We know that this, too, was a concern at the time. This explanation may receive support from the next block of material within the *Book of the Watchers*, which features the ancient figure Enoch, *1 Enoch* 12 – 16.

These chapters report an attempt by the condemned Watchers to use Enoch as a go-between, between themselves and God, to ask for forgiveness and for relief for their offspring. God rejects their petition and instead sends Enoch back to them with a clear and confronting message. "Why have you forsaken the high heaven, the eternal sanctuary; and lain with women, and defiled yourselves with the daughters of men; and taken for yourselves wives, and done as the sons of earth; and begotten for yourselves sons, giants?".[88] Thus here we find a stronger emphasis on their priestly role.

The confrontation continues with the explanation that human beings are mortal, but the Watchers are spirits living forever. Because human beings are mortal, God explains, "therefore I gave them women, that they might cast seed into them, and thus beget children by them, that nothing fail them on earth".[89] Reflecting a very limited notion of sexuality, as having as its sole purpose, propagation, the text then has God declare that because the Watchers "originally

---

[88] *1 Enoch* 15:3.
[89] *1 Enoch* 15:5.

existed as spirits, living forever, and not dying for all the generations of eternity; therefore I did not make women among you".[90] Any sense of sexual relations expressing intimacy and companionship is off the radar.

The message then turns to the fate of the giants. Yes, they died, but their spirits were released into the world, where they continue to wreak havoc, like personified viruses, bacteria and triggers of other ills, plaguing humanity.[91] The message concludes with a reference to that other major threat: men and women who have forbidden knowledge imparted to them by the Watchers: "through this mystery the women and men are multiplying evils on the earth".[92]

The myth of the Watchers was a powerful and, for many, convincing account of the way things are. They found themselves in a world made by God, but invaded by demons and spirits who must be countered at every point, and by human beings who can also be monsters of war or subtle bearers of poisonous ideas and seductions. Good news becomes for such people liberation from such powers. Healers perform exorcisms by God's Spirit. Hope is for the defeat of such demons and their chief, variously described as the devil, Satan, Belial, Beelzuboul, Mastema, and his lieutenants. Jesus' ministry of exorcisms and proclamation of the coming reign of God makes very good sense against this background.

While a gross act of sexual wrongdoing lies at the heart of the myth, it is surprising to find that in neither the actions of the giants, nor those of their spirits, do we find sexual wrongdoing as a feature. In the broadest sense the myth may be targeting marriages with foreigners, perhaps particularly by priests, though this is never explicit. It may be indirectly reflecting on the sexual violence which occurred in warfare, a phenomenon still with us today. The focus overall, however, in describing human ills and wickedness is not on sexual wrongdoing. The myth assumes women were complicit in the original act and so to blame, but beyond that the account of the consequences of the misdeed, unlike the deed itself, seems uninterested in depicting sexual wrongdoing in the present by either women or men as an outcome.

The Watcher Myth in Later Literature

The Watcher myth became influential in many circles of Jewish thought. The *Book of Dream Visions*, part 4 of *1 Enoch*, found in *1 Enoch* 83-90, was written in the first half of the second century B. C. E. Its version of the myth comes in symbolic language, depicting the Watchers as stars. First Asael descended to earth

---

[90] *1 Enoch* 15:6.
[91] *1 Enoch* 15:11.
[92] *1 Enoch* 16:3.

with his forbidden knowledge, then the other stars descended and became bulls with huge penises. These then mounted cows, who gave birth to elephants, camels, and asses. Heaven sent angels to bind the stars and turn the animals to mutual warfare. The author applies the myth to those who are leading the people astray, but also to forbidden intermarriage, probably with Gentiles. Forbidden knowledge again features, but nothing remains of the version in the *Book of the Watchers* about blaming women. Sexual wrongdoing, aside from the primary act, is not in focus. The animals perish in the flood.

In the final two chapters of *1 Enoch* we find an account of Noah's birth.[93] Here, too, the myth plays a role, as Lamech, confronted by his wondrous baby, Noah, fears that it may be an offspring of the Watchers, only to be reassured by Enoch through his father, Methuselah, that all is well and this is not so. The same story reappears in the *Genesis Apocryphon*, a writing recovered from the caves at the Dead Sea.[94]

The book of *Jubilees*, which, as we saw above, produced a creative retelling of the making of woman, also offered an innovative account of the Watcher myth. Drawing on the *Book of the Watchers*, the first section of *1 Enoch*, but perhaps also on other unknown sources, it has the Watchers already on earth, sent there by God to teach.[95] Perhaps its version reflects a setting which, unlike in *1 Enoch*, valued some of the ancient learning. It is only while they are fulfilling their commission that they become engrossed with the women.

The book of *Jubilees* bears its title because it recounts history over 50 *Jubilees* (50 year periods). Seen in this light its placement of the Watchers' misdeed precisely in the twenty-fifth jubilee gives the myth major importance. It closely follows the account in Genesis, but makes the connection between their act and human wickedness more obvious by depicting wrongdoing as corrupting one's way and departing from one's prescribed course. A major concern in *Jubilees* is marriage to Gentiles. By implication, departing from one's prescribed course by marrying and engaging in sexual intercourse with foreigners is comparable to what the angels did with the women. It is to court disaster. While this is doubtless implied, surprisingly in the author's many warnings against intermarriage, he never uses the myth explicitly in this way.

Jubilees has its own reflection on the release of the evil spirits, which, as we saw, the *Book of the Watchers* understood to have come out of the corpses of the slain giants. *Jubilees* simply speaks of these impure demons as children of the Watchers, and identifies their leader as Mastema a word closely related to the word Satan. In an amelioration of what in *1 Enoch* seems rather hopeless, *Jubilees*

---

[93] *1 Enoch* 107–108.

[94] 1QapGen ar/1Q20 2-5.

[95] *Jub.* 5:1-12.

recounts that Noah complained to God about their activity, who agreed to release only 10 per cent of them to roam free.[96] Their roles include, as in *1 Enoch*, being viruses to afflict human beings with pain and illness, against which Noah is taught medicine, but they extend far beyond that to include leadership of nations and enticement to idolatry and intermarriage. In comparison with the myth in the *Book of the Watchers*, *Jubilees* makes no mention of metallurgy, cosmetics and jewellery, apparently deems some of the angelic information legitimate, passed on under divine commission, and does not blame women by making them complicit. Sexual wrongdoing is a major theme in *Jubilees*, but the author does little to exploit the myth of the Watchers in countering it.

The myth reappears in a number of other writings. The *Damascus Document*, found first in two incomplete manuscripts in the Cairo genizah, in synagogue storage, in the early twentieth century, and then in many fragments in Cave 4 of the Dead Sea Scrolls, is a work dating probably from the late second century B. C. E. or shortly thereafter. It makes the Watchers' sin the first of a litany of acts of sexual wrongdoing.[97] The fragmentary first two columns of the *Genesis Apocryphon* give an account of the myth similar to that found in *Jubilees*. Brief references to the myth are found in other documents among the scrolls: in the *Thanksgiving Hymns*, a collection of poems, some of which probably derive from the founder of the Qumran community and reach back into the second century B. C. E. They refer to God's judgement against the Watchers.[98] *4QAges of Creation* refers to the act itself, the leadership of Azazel (replacing Asael), and God's judgement. Some speak of the "bastard spirits" alluding to their origin according to the myth.[99]

The second section in *1 Enoch*, as preserved in the Ethiopic version, the *Parables of Enoch*, is an independent work, written probably around the turn of the millennium. It brings its own reworked version of the myth.[100] While mentioning the Watchers' sexual intercourse with women, the focus falls mainly on their imparting information about metallurgy and the secrets of sorcery under the leadership of Azazel, the renaming of Asael noted above. Metallurgy means weapons of war.[101] There is no mention of jewellery, let alone of enticement by women. The author holds up God's judgement on the Watchers as a warning to rulers of the day, including, probably Herod the Great. In a section concerned with Noah, which may reflect an earlier source, we find some angels named

---

[96] *Jub.* 10:1-14.

[97] CD 2.17-19.

[98] 1QHodayot^a/1QH^a xviii.34b-36.

[99] 4QShir^{a,b}/4Q510, 511; *4QIncantation*/4Q444; 11QapocPs/11Q11.

[100] *1 Enoch* 39:1- 3; 62:9-12; 68:2 – 69:1.

[101] *1 Enoch* 52:1-9.

together with their misdeeds.[102] They include sexual defilement with women and leading their fellows to do so. One is identified as having led Eve astray, but nothing suggests sexual seduction.

2 Enoch, also written around the turn of the millennia, refers to the Watchers' sexual defilement and the birth of the giants,[103] but makes no reference to illicit knowledge, and uses their judgement as a warning against sin in general, not sexual sin, in particular. *2 Baruch* notes that evil women may endanger angels and cites the Watchers' deed and their judgement.[104] The *Apocalypse of Abraham*, with 4 Ezra and *2 Baruch*, representing reflection on the implications of the debacle of the temple's destruction in 70 C. E. for the future, mentions their defilement through sexual wrongdoing,[105] and may allude to the myth in speaking of Azazel's being enamoured with the earth.[106] The myth is the basis for the elaboration of demonology in those chapters of the *Testament of Solomon* which appear to derive from the late first or early second century C. E. In them Beelzeboul claims to be the Watchers' sole survivor.[107] He excites lust for sexual wrongdoing among priests.[108] Other demons perpetrate a range of sexual abuses.

Paul's concern about angels and unveiled women may reflect the myth.[109] The *Wisdom of Solomon*, a sophisticated composition in Greek by an Alexandrian Jew in the early first century C. E. and pseudonymously attributed to king Solomon, knows a version of the myth according to which, unlike in *1 Enoch* and *Jubilees*, the giants were drowned in Noah's flood,[110] a version reflected also in fragments of a work composed in the first half of the second century B. C. E., known as *Pseudo-Eupolemus*, and in Josephus. The latter notes the angels' sexual intercourse with women, compares their offspring, the giants, with their Greek counterparts, and describes them as "completely enslaved to the pleasure of sin".[111] The focus, however, is violence not sexual wrongdoing.

In the *Testaments of the Twelve Patriarchs*, a second century C. E. work, presenting farewell speeches by each of the twelve sons of Jacob, which reflect ethical values merging Jewish and Stoic perspectives, but containing much earlier material, we find a remarkable rewriting of the myth. In the *Testament of Reuben* the author removes the detail of angels having sex with women. Rather they fall

---

[102] *1 Enoch* 69:2-12.
[103] *2 Enoch* 18:1-9.
[104] *2 Bar.* 56:10-13.
[105] *Apoc. Ab.* 24:6.
[106] *Apoc. Ab.* 13:6.
[107] *T. Sol.* 6:1.
[108] *T. Sol.* 6:4.
[109] 1 Cor 11:10.
[110] Wis 14:6.
[111] *A.J.* 1.74.

pregnant to the angels during intercourse with their own husbands: the Watchers "changed themselves into the shape of men, and they appeared to them when they were having sexual intercourse with their husbands. And they, lusting in their mind after their appearances, bore giants; for the Watchers appeared to them as reaching unto heaven".[112] The size may have a phallic reference or may be size in general. The angels are to blame but so are the women. The author has just been describing women as dangerous and as engaging in seductive warfare against men, using ornaments and cosmetics, perhaps an allusion to Asael's influence according to the myth.[113] So they "bewitched the Watchers".[114] The author reports that the Watchers looked at them continually. "They (probably the Watchers and the women) lusted after one another".[115] Such looking at women, he urges, is to be avoided as fateful.

The *Testament of Simeon* may well allude to the myth when it declares that sexual immorality is the mother of all evil and grounds the claim in an appeal to the writings of Enoch.[116] The *Testament of Naphtali* emphasises divine order, citing the Watchers' deed to illustrate disorder, alongside a reference to the men of Sodom engaging in same-sex relations as a further instance.[117]

An exception to the negative portrait of the Watchers' deeds is the account in *Sibylline Oracles* 1 – 2, which depicts them as watchful and inventive.[118] It thus ignores their sexual misdeeds and their forbidden knowledge and, more in the spirit of *Jubilees*, acknowledges that they had been bearers also of legitimate knowledge. In his work *De Gigantibus* ("On Giants") Philo all but ignores the myth in any literal sense, though he mentions the act of sexual wrongdoing, preferring to use it as a basis for allegorical elaboration to address the dangers of the passions, represented in women, and the evil mind, represented in the angels.

In the Beginning?

In this chapter we have looked at two sets of myths. The first is foundational and may be assumed to have been general knowledge among Jews of the period, at least in essence, if not in detail. The creation stories in Genesis 1 – 2 and the account of God's judgement as a result of the sin in the garden in Genesis 3 assured them that creation was good, including being human with all that that entails, and not least sexuality which is directly addressed in these stories.

---

[112] *T. Reub.* 5:6-7.

[113] *1 Enoch* 8:1-2.

[114] *T. Reub.* 5:6.

[115] *T. Reub.* 5:6.

[116] *T. Sim.* 5:3-4.

[117] *T. Naph.* 3:4-5; 4:1.

[118] *Sib. Or.* 1:98-100.

Disobedience and judgement did not undermine that belief, but rather underlined that it was essential to live within God's creation in the way God has ordered it. The stories leave some ambiguities, such as whether female sexual desire and subordination to the male came only as a sentence of judgement, which is less likely, or whether its mention in Gen 3:16 is part of depicting the cycle of painful childbirth. It does not, in any case call sexual desire itself and its expression into question.

The myth of the Watchers provided a basis for reflecting on violence and vulnerability in the world, not least through evil spirits and the suffering imposed by warring nations. While it all went wrong because of an act of sexual wrongdoing which defied divine order, and judgement on its perpetrators served as a warning against defying that order, the myth did not inspire the development of exhortations to avoid such sexual wrongdoing, apart from a few exceptions related to intermarriage. Rather it provided a basis for understanding why violence happens and where evil spirits come from and how to counter them. Despite being about an act of sexual wrongdoing, the myth was not really about sex at all and certainly did not call it into question as long as it followed the divine order of creation.

Households

Households and Livelihood

Very little has survived of the buildings in which people lived in the eastern Mediterranean two thousand years ago. The buildings which have are mostly those of the more wealthy who could afford to build in stone. As the surviving literature, which was also the work of those well-off, indicates, more wealthy families would usually live in a complex household with slaves. Some dwellings reflect that more than one generation lived together, perhaps with a common courtyard.

While ruling powers might demonstrate their presence with occasional intrusions into trouble spots, the agents of power would make their presence felt largely in relation to various forms of taxation or at border crossings. For Judea these were first the Egyptians to the south, ruled over by Alexander the Great's general, Ptolemy and his successors; then after 200 B. C. E. the Seleucid rulers to the north, where Syria was ruled over by another general, Seleucus, and his successors, whose more aggressive interventions were driven by financial constraint; and then after 63 B. C. E. the Romans. Their rule was delegated to puppet governors like Herod the Great, and his successors who ruled over his divided territories, Judea, Galilee, Perea, territories further north east. From 6 C. E. Judea came under direct rule through a Roman prefect, later called a procurator. The temple authorities might also make their presence felt, at least in the collection of tithes and temple taxes.

Daily life for most people entailed making the local economy work, which meant subsistence farming, but also some sale of produce and crafts. Few families were self-sufficient. Most were enmeshed in dependency on the more wealthy, who provided work but also some security in return for it. There was no welfare system run by the state with safety nets for misfortune or disadvantage. To be sick or disabled was to be poor. Charity relief was haphazard, but happened where faith expressed itself in such concerns, either through the local faith community (synagogue) or through special religious movements. The poor, the widow, the orphan, might receive such help. For most, from the more wealthy to the majority who barely eked out a living, help and support was self-made. There were no charities, no health insurance companies, no refuges.

Marriages and Households

When Gen 2:24 speaks of a man leaving his mother and father joining himself to his wife, becoming one flesh with her, it is talking about a new beginning, a new household. It would need to be strong and stable enough to sustain the children which that joining would inevitably bring in a world of inadequate contraception. For this reason most men apparently married at around 30 years of age when they would have gained sufficient to be able to start such a household. It is probably no coincidence that the gospels give this as the age of Jesus when he chose his special path – instead of doing what most others did and marrying.

Men married women who were 10 – 15 years younger. It made sense for fathers to seek to marry off their daughters while they were young. Leaving it too long exposed them to the danger of falling pregnant outside of marriage, which was seen as bringing shame on the father and his household. The view was widespread that women had limited control of their passions and so needed as soon as possible to be harnessed into a stable relationship. Paul reassures anxious fathers that they should not hesitate to let their daughters marry if that seems what is required, and hold back only when there is no such pressure and no prior commitment.[1]

In its exposition of law, the *Damascus Document* addresses the issue of the behaviour of daughters in their father's house or beyond it and emphasises its importance for his being able to make an honest case that they are worthy partners for worthy men.[2] It stresses that the father must be honest about blemishes of his daughter and choose a suitable partner[3] and uses the rules about inappropriate mixing of seed and cloth[4] to argue also for fathers making the right choices for their sons. It forbids marriage to an immoral unmarried woman, an immoral woman beyond her father's house (probably meaning an adulteress and therefore, divorced), and a widow who has not remained chaste.[5] By implication marriage to

---

[1] 1 Cor 7:36-38.
[2] 4QD^e/4Q270 2 i.16-17a; 4QD^f/4Q271 3 8-16; similarly 4QInstr^a/4Q415 11 and 4QInstr^d/4Q418 167b.
[3] 4QD^f/4Q271 3 8-16.
[4] Deut 22:10-11.
[5] 4QD^e/4Q270 2 i.17.

an unmarried woman, to a divorcee who is not an adulteress (such as one whose husband the community has expelled for illicit intercourse, probably reported by her), and to a chaste widow, is acceptable.

Some concerns about daughters seem extreme. Such is the case with the Wisdom of Jesus Ben Sira, a work written in Hebrew in the early second century B. C. E. by a teacher and sage and translated into Greek later in the century by his grandson. He, for instance, claims that since daughters are barely able to contain their sexual passions, left unchecked, they are likely to engage in indiscriminate sexual behaviour.[6] They are, he somewhat crudely suggests, like quivers going about looking for arrows,[7] and so should be kept out of sight of men and away from experienced women who might corrupt their thoughts.[8] Daughters are not to parade their beauty before men.[9] Ben Sira warns against seducing virgins, but the appeal appears to be based on self-interest: the likely fine her father might impose.[10]

His worries do not stop there. Married women are also vulnerable to their passions, falling to infidelity and so becoming "hated", a common term for divorce,[11] thus bringing shame on their fathers. In his view a wicked man is still preferable to a good woman.[12] A wicked wife should, accordingly be locked away.[13] A quarrelsome one is like a shaking yoke,[14] and likely to get out of control, engage in adulterous relations and bring illegitimate heirs into the family which would threaten the household's future,[15] like an uncontrollable flow of water.[16] A wife should be submissive and silent, not loud and garrulous.[17] She should not be wealthier or more resourceful than her husband, setting him in dependence on her.[18] That would shame a man and his children as much as one who engages directly in wickedness.[19] Ben Sira writes of woman as the source of men's woes, perhaps alluding to Eve, but in any case generalising it to all women.[20] His negative portrait may well draw on a particular reading of Gen 3:16

---

[6] Sir 42:9-14; 26:10-12, perhaps originally of wives; cf. also 26:7-9; 25:25-26.

[7] Sir 26:12.

[8] Sir 42:11-13.

[9] Sir 42:12.

[10] Sir 9:5.

[11] Sir 42:9.

[12] Sir 42:14.

[13] Sir 42:6.

[14] Sir 26:7.

[15] Sir 23:22-26.

[16] Sir 25:25-26.

[17] Sir 26:23-27; 25:25-26.

[18] Sir 25:22.

[19] Sir 3:11b; 23:22-26; 26:7-9.

[20] Sir 25:24.

as indicating that women cannot help themselves but must blindly pursue their sexual desires.

Such fears are by no means confined to Ben Sira, even though expressed more moderately elsewhere. Aristotle's assessment was that a woman has inferior reasoning power to a man, and was, in effect, "a defective male",[21] a view also set out in Plato's creation account, who saw women and then animals as progressively more defective beings resulting from failure at the higher (male) level.[22] Such views, which made the rounds of popular philosophical discourse, will have reinforced[23] for some the belief that women should be tightly controlled[23] and daughters kept indoors and out of sight.[24] *Pseudo-Phocylides* has similar advice. It is a work of 231 lines written in sophisticated Greek hexameters in Ionic dialect and claiming to be work of the sixth or seventh B. C. E Miletian philosopher, Phocylides, but, as its vocabulary, style, and content shows, was authored by a Jew somewhere between the mid first century B. C. E. and the mid first century C. E. *Pseudo-Phocylides* advises: "Guard a virgin in closely shut chambers, and let her not be seen before the house until her wedding day. The beauty of children is hard for parents to protect".[25] Seclusion indoors presumes wealthy settings with multi-roomed houses. The romance, *Joseph and Aseneth*, composed as entertainment with ethical intent for a Jewish audience in Egypt some time in the first centuries B. C. E. or C. E., has the virgin Ascneth cooped up in a tower, untouched and unseen except by seven virgin assistants.[26] According to the *Testaments of the Twelve Patriarchs*, men should exercise strict control over both their wives and daughters to prevent them from equipping themselves with the weaponry of adornment and cosmetics.[27]

Not all was hopeless. The heroic woman of 4 Maccabees, and Susanna in the legend which bears her name, composed in Hebrew probably late second or early second century B. C. E. and preserved as an appendix to Daniel, depict women able, unlike Eve in the Greek version of the garden of Eden, to resist the snake's seduction.[28]

Thus people saw right order being followed when men around 30 married women some 10-15 years younger. Men thus took primary responsibility for their young wives, who for a range of reasons, including age, experience, and, sometimes, ideology, were deemed inferior. It was common advice that men

---

[21] Aristotle *Gen. an.* 737A.28.

[22] Plato, *Timaeus*, 42B, 91A.

[23] *Ps.-Arist.* 250-251.

[24] 2 Macc 3:19-20; similarly 3 Macc 1:18; 4 Macc 18:7; Philo *Spec.* 3.169.

[25] *Ps.-Phoc.* 215-217.

[26] *Asen.* 2:1-12.

[27] *T. Reub.* 5:5.

[28] 4 Macc 18:7-10; cf. also *LAB* 13:8; Wis 14:4.

should see one of their roles as educating their wives, particularly for household responsibilities. Normally women were in charge of domestic affairs and men of external matters. In a relatively wealthy household with slaves that would entail that a woman would need to develop skills of both personnel and resource management. It could sometimes occur that a widow might continue to run a household single-handed after premature death of her spouse. This way widows and orphans might inherit wealth.[29]

Judith is a celebrated example. Her legend is told in the writing bearing her name, composed in Hebrew probably in the first half of the first century B. C. E., and preserved in Greek translation. She was head of her household after her husband's untimely death,[30] but in addition stepped into national leadership when the men were at their wits' end, and rescued the people from danger. At great personal risk, like the legendary Jael before her,[31] she used her sexual attractiveness to trap and defeat Holofernes.[32] Her act of leadership was one-off; she returned to her household leadership, which was also exceptional, but remained within the overall framework of patriarchal society.[33] Her story may well have served those who tried to bolster support for Queen Salome Alexandra, who rose to be queen over Israel after the death of her husband Alexander Janneus in 76 B. C. E. The historian Josephus reports her rise and her close collaboration with the Pharisees against their rivals the Sadducees, though he cannot help himself commenting that her gender was not befitting for such leadership, a sentiment expressed by her son who succeeded her and reversed her allegiances.[34]

While women may be depicted as taking important initiatives in marriages, such partnerships were far from equal. Tobit, in the legend bearing his name, was always wiser than Anna, though he was not always right.[35] Similarly Job in the *Testament of Job*, a work composed in Greek around the turn of the millennium, was always wiser than Sitidos, who still warranted sympathy from hearers. Sitidos' compassionate support of Job exposed her to significant danger.[36]

There were celebrated stories of women exercising leadership, though often that was depicted as their acting like men, as with the heroic mother in 4 Maccabees who showed "manly courage".[37] Some writers appear to have gone out of their way to emphasise women heroes. *Jubilees* gives particular prominence to

---

[29] 2 Macc 3:10.

[30] Jdt 8:3.

[31] Judges 4.

[32] Jdt 10 – 13.

[33] Jdt 16:23.

[34] *A.J.* 13.417, 430-31.

[35] Tob 2:14-15.

[36] *T. Job.* 23:7-9.

[37] 4 Macc 14:11.

Rebecca, who is shown to run rings around her staid husband, Isaac. The same kind of emphasis is found in the *Book of Biblical Antiquities*, sometimes called *Pseudo-Philo*, and abbreviated from its Latin title, *Liber Antiquitatum Biblicarum* as *LAB*, a work composed in Hebrew in the first century C. E., surviving in a Latin translation of a Greek version. It has Amram cite Tamar, Judah's daughter-in-law, who acted as a prostitute to become pregnant by him rather than by a foreigner, as a model, describing her as "our mother" as Abraham is our father.[38] It depicts Jephthah's daughter, Seila, as a new Isaac,[39] celebrates Deborah as a "mother from Israel"[40] and praises Jael's feat of executing the enemy army chief, Sisera, after seducing him, a deed which foreshadowed Judith's execution of the general, Holofernes.[41] That author nevertheless still declares in relation to Deborah that to be ruled by a woman was shameful and merited God's punishment.[42] The underlying sentiment is that it is a sign of failure if men are ruled by women, since the reverse should always be the case. It was even worse for a man to be slain by a woman, as happened in the exploits of Jael[43] or Judith;[44] or to die like one.[45] So there was room for women heroes, in politics, war, or religion, as in Job's daughters who became prophets,[46] but it was not the expected norm.

The apparently dichotomous view of women is just as evident in the early Christian movement, where beside affirmation of charismatic women exercising leadership, more especially in the earlier years, very evident among those named by Paul as fellow leaders,[47] we find instructions that apply to normal life, which include that women should retain their traditional roles and dress. Thus women are not to abandon their veils in worship, according to Paul, for he sees the veil as part of what by divine order it means to be a woman.[48] That includes when they exercise leadership such as in public prayer and prophecy. Paul's stance reflects his society but he provides a rationale on the basis of his reading of the Greek translation of Genesis, which allows one to see women as in the image of men and men in the image of God.[49] That is simply the way things are, as he sees it.

---

[38] *LAB* 9:5.

[39] *LAB* 32:5.

[40] *LAB* 33:6.

[41] *LAB* 31:3-9; cf. Jdt 12:15.

[42] *LAB* 30:2.

[43] *LAB* 31:1, 9; Judg 4:9.

[44] Jdt 9:10; 13:15; 16:6.

[45] *Asen.* 25:7.

[46] *T. Job.* 46-50.

[47] So Rom 16:3-16.

[48] 1 Cor 11:2-16.

[49] 1 Cor 11:2-3.

At the same time and for the same reason he can protest against any diminution of women's value, pointing out, perhaps also playfully, that as woman came from man (Eve from Adam), so every man comes from a woman.[50] Earlier, writing to the Galatians, he had penned the affirmation that "there is neither Jew nor Greek, slave nor free, male and female, for you are all one in Christ Jesus".[51] All are to be valued, but in the light of his expositions of such thought elsewhere it is clear that he is not advocating that people abandon their distinctiveness. Rather, they should have a sense of belonging. Slaves should stay slaves, especially given what he saw as the limitations of time as the world approached its end and Christ's coming, and avail themselves of freedom only where the opportunity arises.[52] Women should certainly not try to be like men, but remain faithfully in their place.

When addressing the normal situation where men and women come together, Paul is quite clear. They should follow what would be normal public decorum and remain silent, waiting till later to ask their husbands questions which might arise in their minds.[53] While there were exceptions, these were not to be the model for normal ordering, which to Paul is of great importance. In some of his churches, such as in Corinth, there may have been other influences driving women's assertiveness reflecting Roman trends. There had been a shift in marriage custom from the common assumption that a father passes authority over his daughter to her husband. In Paul's time it was common for the father's authority to remain, even after marriage, which had as a side effect that many women gained greater freedom and we know that there was some unrest at the extent to which this occurred. Perhaps Corinth, strongly influenced by Roman culture, was a setting where even Christian congregations experienced such assertiveness.

But already within the movement itself there was a strong emphasis on acceptance and belonging as something applying to all, including those often shunned as of lesser worth, among whom were women, Gentiles, slaves, not to speak of various "sinners". It was a stance which had its roots in the ministry of Jesus, where it was applied primarily to his fellow Jews, but soon compelled a reassessment of treatment of non-Jews. A message of such belonging threatened to call into question the structures which subordinated some to others. Such outbreaks of radical thought needed to be brought under control. So in Paul we see a simmering tension between commitment to what he believed was divine order and a value system which had the potential to overthrow it.

Proper order and behaviour became all the more important as the new movement became exposed to the eyes of the moral critics of society. The author of 1 Peter, writing in the name of the great apostle, cautions the Christian

---

[50] 1 Cor 11:11-12.
[51] Gal 3:28.
[52] 1 Cor 7:21.
[53] 1 Cor 14:33b-36.

community to conform to what were the best and noble ideals of society.[54] It had no business and no need to subvert the structures of society. Its challenge was to live faithfully within them and to commend its faith as good news for the community in the face of its sometimes violent responses. Earlier two different authors claimed Paul's authority in issuing instructions about the proper ordering of family life in accordance with what was seen as best practice in the world of the time.[55] We recognise the social norms in the exhortation that wives obey husbands, husbands treat them well; that children obey their parents and fathers (in control of the boys) not discourage them; and that slaves obey masters and masters not abuse them. Similar sets of rules appear also in *Pseudo-Phocylides*.[56] In their Christianised form we again find the tension between established order and individual worth, as appeals are made to Christ's behaviour, especially his love, which would along with other complex influences many centuries later undermine the structural inequalities. At the same time we see Christian tradition employed to bolster the accepted order. Christ is made the example for the husband, the church for the bride.[57] It would have been unthinkable to reverse these and see Christ as the model for the wife and the church for the husband, not just because Christ is male, but also because it would have contravened the hierarchy of Christ over the church as husband over the wife.

The tension is already evident when reading the anecdotes which have survived in the gospels about Jesus' attitudes towards women. Without question a controversial aspect of his ministry was his reversal of the norms which many espoused. That included his willingness to reach out to people considered outcasts through no fault of their own or who had made themselves outcasts, among them both men and women. He was among those Jews who affirmed women and did not deem them dangerous and needing to be controlled or avoided like Ben Sira. Women feature in the early stories claiming his resurrection,[58] reflecting that they will have been well integrated among his followers during his ministry, as Mark reports.[59] On the other hand, the twelve, chosen in part to symbolise Israel, are all male, as one would have expected within society of the time. The women do not disappear, so that we hear incidentally in Paul of some who exercised leadership,[60] but they were exceptions within what was a male oriented world. It does not serve the interests of the equality which we today want to uphold to deny this history.

---

[54] 1 Pet 2:11 – 3:7.

[55] Col 3:18 – 4:1; Eph 5:21 – 6:9.

[56] *Ps.-Phoc.* 175-227.

[57] Eph 5:25-33.

[58] Mark 16:1-8; Matt 28:1-10; Luke 24:1-12; John 20:1-18.

[59] Mark 15:40-41.

[60] Rom 16:3-16.

Arranging Marriages

Marriage was not a private affair, as it has become in the western world. It was a concern of the local community, and especially of the extended family. The welfare of the family was at stake. It was in everyone's interests to ensure that the marriage would work and households be viable. Children were a blessing in more senses than one. They would become an important source of labour and then of support for their aging parents, if they survived to old age, though not many did. So marriages were arranged between families, normally within the extended family. Wise heads could then assess compatibility and likely future prospects.

In Roman society there was also a preference for marrying within the extended family or clan, unlike in Greek culture which encouraged marriage beyond those parameters. An exception is Pericles' decree of 451 B. C. E. that Athenian citizens were to marry only Athenians.[61] Roman society was complex, with layers of class structure: the senatorial class, the equestrian class, the plebs (ordinary citizens), freedmen and women, and various ranks of slaves. Normally one should marry within one's class. Proper order was essential for both the state and the household and the man must be in control.

Household order and security had to be a high priority across all three cultures. One can understand the anxiety expressed in Ben Sira about keeping a careful watch over daughters. Dating as we might know it among teenagers had no place. Pairing was something for the family to decide not the whims of romantic attraction. Of course, the conflict of interests had the potential to spawn all kinds of dramas. As in societies today where marriages are arranged, wise heads can often make a match where love and affection grows. They may even have read the signs of love in the first place.

There are many stories about finding the right partner. We see them in Genesis with Abraham's sending his trusted servants to find the right wife for Isaac[62] and Jacob's travelling to Laban's family.[63] The book of Tobit makes it the main story. Tobit insists that his son Tobias must marry within his own extended family – even claiming it as divinely mandated.[64] There was debate about the rules, including whether priests could marry outside priestly families and whether Jews could marry proselytes or Gentiles who did not convert. We shall discuss these in the context of purity issues in the next chapter.

---

[61] Aristotle *Ath. Pol.* 26.4; Plutarch, *Pericles* 37.2-5.
[62] Gen 24:1-9.
[63] Gen 28:1-5.
[64] Tob 4:12-13.

Limitations

Within the extended family there were also limits to be observed. Leviticus 18 frames them in terms of incest, prohibiting sexual intercourse between parent or step-parent and child or grandchild, including their spouses; brother and sister (including step-siblings) and their spouses; and nephew and aunt. According to Mark, John the Baptist was executed because he objected to Antipas marrying his step-brother's divorced wife.[65] In polygynous marriages Leviticus forbids marrying a mother and her daughter; and two living sisters. Jacob did the latter in marrying Leah and Rachel, but was tricked into it.[66] *Jubilees* offers heavenly sanction, at least for the sequence of marrying the elder sister first.[67] The *Testaments of the Twelve Patriarchs* ignore the anomaly.[68]

Controversy raged over whether the prohibition of marrying a nephew implied a similar prohibition against marrying one's niece. The *Temple Scroll*, found among the writings of the Dead Sea Scrolls and written probably some time in the second century B. C. E., assumes it does, but without portraying it as an issue of contention.[69] The book of *Jubilees* worries that Abraham married his niece, as some appear to have read Gen 11:29, identifying Sarah with his niece, Isaca, as did Josephus later,[70] so opts for the lesser offence in its view of making Sarah his sister[71] and where possible elsewhere adjusts genealogies to remove "good" people from such relationships. The *Damascus Document*, was written at a time when the matter was clearly contentious and declares niece marriages an act of sexual immorality.[72] That view was later shared by the Sadducees, a strongly priestly group within the Jerusalem establishment during this period.

Opposing them were the Pharisees who reasoned that Leviticus forbad only marriage to nephews, not marriage to nieces, which they, or at least their successors, the rabbis, saw in very positive terms.[73] The *Aramaic Levi Document*, stemming probably from the third century B. C. E. and the related work, the *Visions of Amram*, from probably a century later, have no qualms in mentioning not only niece marriages,[74] but that Amram, Moses' father, had married his aunt,

---

[65] Mark 6:18.

[66] Gen 29:15-30.

[67] *Jub.* 28:6; cf. Gen 29:26.

[68] Cf. *T. Iss.* 1 – 2.

[69] 11QT^a/11Q19 66.15-16.

[70] *A.J.* 1.151.

[71] *Jub.* 12:9.

[72] CD 5.7b-11a; similarly 4QD^e/4Q270 2 ii.16; *4QHalakha A*/4Q251 17 2, 4-5.

[73] *t. Qidd.* 1.4; *b. Yebam.* 62b-63a; *b. Sanh.* 76b.

[74] *ALD* 11:1 / 62; 4Q543 1a-c 5-6 = 4Q545 1a i.5-6 = 4Q546 1 3-4.

Jochabed,[75] a detail preserved already in Exod 6:20 and Num 26:59 and contravening Lev 18:12; 20:19, and which *Jubilees* seeks to minimise by omission. The *Testaments of the Twelve Patriarchs* may be seeking to ameliorate the situation by reporting that both Jochabed and Amram were born on the same day.[76]

Greco-Roman cultures also had limitations on whom one might marry. Generally marriage to nieces was forbidden, although it did sometimes occur when the sole surviving child was a daughter and the only option was for an uncle to marry her. There is some evidence of acceptance of marriage of siblings in our period, including the marriage of Ptolemy 2 Philadelphus to his sister Arsenoe 2, which no evidence indicates was a reflection of any Egyptian influence. As noted above, for the author of *Jubilees* it was preferable to have Abraham marry Sarah as his sister than as his niece.

Marrying

The book of Tobit, despite its fairy tale character, helps us trace the steps which lead to a marriage. A negotiation must take place between the groom's father and the father of the bride, either directly or through the former's representative. Finding wives for sons was a major responsibility and, if it could not be done by fathers, someone else had to assume responsibility. We see this also when Zebul arranges husbands for the daughters of Kenaz in Pseudo-Philo.[77] In Tobit's case an angel in human form represents him.[78] The woman in question is Sarah, daughter of Tobit's kinsman, Raguel. The negotiations confirm that Sarah qualifies, that is, belongs to Tobias' kin.[79]

Raguel places her hand in Tobias' hand, and in this act gives her to Tobias, and wishes him peace as he takes her to his father, Tobit.[80] This reflects the norm that the woman passes from the hands of one man to another's and also that she passes into the father's side of the extended family. A contract is signed which puts his giving away Sarah in writing according to the law of Moses and a celebration begins.[81] She retires to a room to await Tobias.[82] Finally Tobias comes and they consummate the marriage.[83] A feast follows before Tobias and Sarah return to

---

[75] *ALD* 12:3 / 75.

[76] *T. Levi* 12:4.

[77] *LAB* 29:2.

[78] Tob 5:4-8.

[79] Tob 7:1-10.

[80] Tob 7:11-14; 10:10-13.

[81] Tob 7:13-14.

[82] Tob 7:15.

[83] Tob 8:1-9.

Tobit, together with a substantial dowry given by Raguel.[84] The new marriage builds new relationships, which include honouring one's parents-in-law as much as one's own and reciprocal recognition of a new son or daughter.[85]

In the tale the meeting and the marriage, everything, happens overnight. In most circumstances there would be a gap between the agreement between the fathers and the wedding, for which there would need to be preparation. That interim period may be designated a betrothal, although its legal standing is unclear. The agreement would need to be sufficiently secure to be able to proceed with arrangements. In the case of Mary and Joseph in the story of Jesus' birth the time of "betrothal" is assumed to be some months.[86] Paul's discussion of marriage includes reference to situations where there may be a prior agreement to marry which would need to be respected.[87]

From marriage contracts which have survived at Elephantine in Egypt from the fifth century B. C. E., and the Judean desert caves, from the early second century C. E., we see that contracts mainly regulated matters like what happened with money and possessions in the case of death or divorce and occasionally set rules of behaviour in relation to others, including such issues as whether taking a second wife would be acceptable. Not all marriages would have written contracts, especially among the many poor, but for others they mattered, especially those with possessions.

Normally the wife brought into the marriage a dowry of money or kind or both. It was then at the disposal of the husband, but would have to be repaid should the marriage collapse; or an equivalent set sum. Inevitably, greed for large dowries played a role in some men's ambitions, especially where they had become sufficiently independent to take their own initiatives. More than one wife multiplied the benefit. It could also be a trap if confronted by the need to pay dowries back, as could marrying a woman with a substantial dowry.[88] When Luke locates Jesus' prohibition of divorce and remarriage in the context of warnings about monetary greed,[89] he may well have had such men in mind. Greed for wealth appears to be closely associated with the attack on polygyny in the *Damascus Document* for the same reason.[90]

Traditionally the man also gave a gift of money or kind to the wife's family, sometimes called a bride price, but in our period it was probably more by way of making a contribution to the cost of the festivities surrounding the wedding, which

---

[84] Tob 8:21; 10:10; cf. 2 Macc 1:14.

[85] Tob 8:21; 10:12.

[86] Matt 1:18.

[87] 1 Cor 7:36.

[88] *Ps.-Phoc.* 199-203; cf. Sir 25:21; Josephus *Ap.* 2.200; *T. Jud.* 13:4-8.

[89] Luke 16:18; cf. 16:1-15, 19-31.

[90] CD 4.17 – 5.19a; cf. 6.15; 8.5/19.17.

would have been substantial. We do not find the notion that wives could be bought and therefore sold, though the man's contribution is sometimes referred to as the bride price.

How weddings were celebrated is left largely to our imagination. Apparently the bride could be dressed like a queen. *Joseph and Aseneth* pictures the bride dressed in a white robe with veil and sceptre.[91] The Book of Revelation also speaks of a white robe,[92] as does Seila's lament in Pseudo-Philo, couched in imagery recalling Sophocles' *Antigone* and Euripides' *Iphegeneia*. There we find reference to wedding garlands, a white wedding dress, sweet smelling ointment and anointing oil prepared by her mother, a plaited crown of flowers, and a coverlet woven of hyacinth and purple.[93] Rabbinic tradition, too, depicts brides as dressed like queens.[94]

Aseneth's preparation for the wedding included washing,[95] which appears to have been a regular practice in wedding preparation in the wider world.[96] There may have been ritual acts on the wedding night. Both Philo and Josephus mention sacrifices, perhaps a rite to ward off demons, as in Tobit.[97]

As unlikely marriage celebrant, Pharaoh, according to *Joseph and Aseneth*, announces that the couple were destined for each other, declares them man and wife, seats Aseneth on Joseph's right, lays hands on both their heads, blesses them, wishes them fruitfulness and then has them kiss.[98] A feast follows. In the collection of documents found in the caves of the Dead Sea there was what appears to be a document related to wedding ritual. It contains reference to acts of blessing, hope of fertility, and joy in sexual intimacy.[99]

The parable of the ten girls in Matthew[100] assumes, as does the tale of Tobias and Sarah,[101] that the bride withdraws and awaits the groom and depicts his coming as greeted with lamps. This, too, appears to have been a fairly standard pattern of events. Under these circumstances not all husbands remained sober. In this way Josephus accounts for Jacob's sleeping with Leah without knowing it.[102]

---

[91] *Asen.* 15:10; 18:5-6.

[92] Rev 21:3.

[93] *LAB* 40:6.

[94] E.g. *m. Sot.* 9.14.

[95] *Asen.* 18:8.

[96] Cf. also Eph 5:26.

[97] Philo *Spec.* 3.80; Josephus *A.J.* 4.245; Tob 8:2.

[98] *Asen.* 21:6-7.

[99] 4QpapRitMar/4Q502.

[100] Matt 25:1-13.

[101] Tob 7:15-16.

[102] *A.J.* 1.301; cf. Gen 29:23.

He suggests a similar state of drunkenness as the context of Samson's riddle at his marriage feast.[103] Never a promising beginning.

Before Marriage

The available evidence appears to suggest that future couples were not to engage in sexual intercourse until they were married, at least in Jewish society. This is Ben Sira's assumption, who fears pregnancy might ensue, bringing, as he puts it shame on the family and its male head[104] and undermining trust in keeping fidelity in marriage. For this reason he urges men to marry young,[105] something they could do if they had the means. Pre-marital chastity is clearly assumed in the story of Sarah and Tobias in the book of Tobit; there was no time for that to be an issue. It is also emphasised as being the case in Joseph's marriage to Aseneth in *Joseph and Aseneth*.[106] *Jubilees* has Jacob declare to Rebecca his mother, that he had not only kept himself chaste, but for all his 63 years had never even touched a woman.[107] The story of Joseph and Mary assumes pre-marital chastity; otherwise Joseph could never know that the child was not his.[108] Paul's advice about marrying if one cannot exercise self-control[109] reflects similar assumptions as does his assurance to the Corinthians that he wants to present them as a "chaste virgin" to Christ, to whom he had promised them in marriage, and so does not want them to be seduced like Eve, by false teachers.[110]

The provision for dealing with accusations by a husband that his wife was not a virgin similarly assumes she should have been. Thus it allows as (dubitable) proof the producing of a sheet showing blood resulting from the rupture of the hymen on first intercourse.[111] Subsequent discussions of the provision similarly assume virginity at marriage as required. We find it discussed, for instance, in the *Temple Scroll*.[112] It also undergoes significant revision in legal discussion in the documents among the Dead Sea Scrolls. Two expositions dropped the dubitable evidence of blood on sheets (one could easily falsify that evidence) and instead institute a team of senior female inspectors to examine the woman either before or

---

[103] *A.J.* 5.289.

[104] Sir 26:12; 42:9-14; similarly Tob 3:14-15; cf. *Sib. Or.* 2:280-281.

[105] *Asen.* 7:23.

[106] *Asen.* 21:1.

[107] *Jub.* 25:4.

[108] Matt 1:18-19.

[109] 1 Cor 7:8-9.

[110] 2 Cor 11:2-3.

[111] Deut 22:13-19.

[112] 11QTᵃ/11Q19 65.7-15.

after the wedding night.[113] Both Philo and Josephus similarly omit the evidence from blood stains, but both emphasise that the issue is not just about the woman but about her guardians.[114]

While pre-marital chastity was expected, at least officially, of both the man and the woman, the emphasis was primarily on the woman. She was expected to be a virgin at her first marriage. Paul typically reflects the common assumption that women's virginity mattered more when he depicts only unmarried women and virgins as seeking to be holy in body and spirit, something not said similarly of men.[115] At a practical level a woman's virginity would assure a man that she was not already pregnant to someone else, but also that she was likely to be able to exercise the same level of self-control in remaining chaste as a wife. In any case contraception, where attempted, was well nigh impossible and at least unreliable.

As noted above, fathers were urged to ensure their daughters retained their virginity, even if that meant keeping them as far as possible from public view, at least from men's eyes. We may assume that given the cultural expectations of arranged marriages social pressure would have discouraged having liaisons with men in public and without parental approval. Such norms are likely to have been standard in local communities, including among the poor, much as they remain so in many cultures still today.

The practical reasons for not engaging in sexual relations before marriage made more sense for women than for men. There was nothing comparable to pregnancy or ruptured hymens which would expose men's unchastity. So despite the ideals and affirmations, it would have been very likely that men sought sexual experience before marriage, especially given that they did not marry until they were around 30 years of age. The *Testaments of the Twelve Patriarchs* make a number of references to that ideal age,[116] which happened to be Reuben's age when he raped Bilhah.[117] It finds additional confirmation in the case of Levi's advice to his descendants that they should seek to marry young as he did, namely when he was aged 28.[118] The author even has suggestions about how young men might cope till then. They should keep busy reading literature,[119] and work so hard as farmers that they have no energy left for sex or even for thinking about it and should wait for God to find them a woman in due course.[120] Being busy in the garden helped Adam and Eve deal with abstinence in the garden of Eden,

---

[113] 4QD^f/4Q271 3 13b-15a and 4QOrd^a/4Q159.

[114] Philo *Spec.* 3.79-82; Josephus *A.J.* 4.246-248.

[115] 1 Cor 7:34.

[116] *T. Iss.* 3:5; *T. Levi* 11:8; cf. 12:4.

[117] *T. Reub.* 1:8.

[118] *T. Levi* 9:10; 11:1; 12:5.

[119] *T. Reub.* 4:1.

[120] *T. Reub.* 4:1; similarly *T. Iss.* 3:5; 4:1, 4; *T. Levi* 9:9-10.

according to *Jubilees*, which it depicts as a holy place.[121] For those who did not refrain, the options were few. They included engaging with prostitutes. We return to the issue of prostitution in chapter 4.

Sex and the Household

Ben Sira not only insisted that wives remain chaste, their mouth/vagina sealed,[122] the model of a "sensible" wife,[123] the ideal of the "wife with (her) husband",[124] but he also taught that the husband should keep himself exclusively for her.[125] Adultery on his part is an offence not just against another man by theft of his property, his wife, but also an offence against his own wife, his own "bed".[126] At the very least in the interests of producing legitimate heirs they were to keep themselves only for their wives.[127] Similarly Josephus insisted that sexual intimacy be confined to the relationship between husband and wife.[128] Both seem, however, to have taken an atypical stance. For the usual understanding appears to have been that a man would have sexual access to all in his household, or, in the case of Jews, at least all women except those forbidden in incest laws. Within Jewish tradition that norm was both evident and at the same time beset with strict limitations. Thus in the stories of Abraham and Jacob we see sexual access not only to wives but also to slaves, in their case with the consent and encouragement of the wives.[129]

Jewish law had provisions dealing with sexual access to slaves.[130] It forbad sexual access to another man's slaves, just as it did to another man's wife, but not to his own slaves. It was a matter of discussion among interpreters of the Law. Fragmentary remains of the legal section of the *Damascus Document* indicate discussion of three elements: sex with another's slave, one's own, and a captive woman.[131] As already noted, the practice of sexual access to one's own slaves is assumed in the stories of Abraham and of Jacob, where both are depicted as engaging in intercourse with their wives' maidservants, though at their behest. Ben Sira is exceptional in opposing the practice, at least in the Hebrew, which

---

[121] *Jub.* 3:35.
[122] Sir 26:15b MS C.
[123] Sir 25:8.
[124] Sir 40:23.
[125] Sir 36:24-27.
[126] Sir 23:18.
[127] Sir 26:19-21.
[128] *Ap.* 2.201.
[129] Gen 16:1-6; 30:1-13.
[130] Lev 19:20-22; 21:1-11; Deut 21:10-14.
[131] 4QD^e/4Q270 4 13-19.

presumably preserves what he originally wrote: "[Be ashamed of] meddling [with a maidservant] of *yours*, and of violating her bed".[132] Interestingly his grandson modified that strictness when translating the work into Greek so that in conformity with biblical law it read as a prohibition of sex with another's slave: "of meddling with *his* maidservant, and do not approach her bed".[133]

The extent to which in Jewish households and early Christian households men continued to see themselves as having sexual access to their slaves is uncertain. It is revealing that in discussing the law concerning rape of an unmarried woman, Philo argues that one should not do so because it is the way one treats one's slaves.[134] Where one might have expected it to be addressed, such as in accounts of household order, in *Pseudo-Phocylides*, Colossians and Ephesians, nothing is said. Beyond that one can only surmise that where householders had espoused an ethic of love and respect for all people, at least no sexual abuse of slaves would take place.

Josephus agreed with Herod in deploring the fact that Herod's brother Pheroras fell in love with his slave, and, even more shamefully, married her.[135] Roman law forbad marriage to slaves and to former prostitutes, who were often slaves, and Josephus alleges that Jewish law conforms to this.[136] Philo, on the other hand, sees only priests forbidden to marry prostitutes, not ordinary Israelites.[137]

Times of conquest where women were taken prisoner might result in incorporation of such women into a household, including by marriage. It was sufficiently common to require legislation[138] and revisions of legislation, such as we see in the *Temple Scroll* and the *Damascus Document*.[139] Such women were extremely vulnerable. The biblical law provides such women freedom from sexual exploitation for a month after which they are at the disposal of their captor who can choose either to keep or dismiss them. Such captives, likely to be Gentiles, may well have proved a source of controversy among those who opposed intermarriage with foreigners, an issue we address in the next chapter. The *Damascus Document* assumes that such Gentile slaves could be incorporated into the covenant of Israel, clearly on the assumption that they have adopted the faith of their household. Josephus, clearly embarrassed by the tales of patriarchs engaging in what in Roman eyes was illegal sex with slaves, transforms them into

---

[132] Sir 41:22ab MS B.

[133] Sir 41:24ab.

[134] *Spec.* 3.69.

[135] *A.J.* 16.194, 198; 17.42.

[136] *A.J.* 4.244-245.

[137] *Spec.* 1.101-102.

[138] Deut 21:10-14.

[139] 11QT^a/11Q19 63.10-15; 4QD^e/4Q270 4.19.

the slightly more respectable category of concubines.[140] He reports that Vespasian forced him to take a captive woman as wife, but hastens to add that she was a virgin, so that he would not have contravened rules forbidding priests marrying such women.[141] One would have to assume that when the *Temple Scroll* writes of captive women, almost certainly Gentiles, becoming part of priests' households, that they, too, would be virgins,[142] a practice which would seem to be diametrically opposed by the author of *4QMMT*.[143] This work, found in multiple copies in Cave 4 among the Dead Sea Scrolls, appears to belong to the beginnings of the conflicts which resulted in separation of the leaders of the community from the Jerusalem authorities to settle eventually at Qumran. It probably derived from the late second century B. C. E.

Polygyny

The patriarchal marriages were polygamous, or better polygynous, since the pattern was for men to have more than one wife (*gyne*), not for a woman to have more than one husband. Occasionally we are given a window into what living in a polygynous marriage might mean. The book of *Jubilees* describes how Jacob was in love with Rachel, the woman he had wanted to marry in the first place, but engaged in intercourse also with her sister Leah, and then with the slaves of both for the purpose of producing offspring.[144] Rachel's sterility in no way barred her from sexual relations with Jacob. On the contrary she was the primary lover. Later *Jubilees* describes how Leah became the darling.[145] Accounts of that marriage include stories of negotiation between the wives about sexual access to Jacob.[146] In a similar way Philo contrasts the sexual relationship between Abraham and Sarah and Abraham and Hagar, her slave, depicting the former as full of love and the latter as purely functional.[147]

Ben Sira proffers advice about dealing with rivalry among wives, noting that it can create serious problems for husbands.[148] Such rivalry is likely to have included conflict over sexually related issues and fertility, as in Jacob's marriage. *Pseudo-Philo* depicts rivalries between Manoah and Eluma, in Samson's family of

---

[140] *A.J.* 1.307-308; *LAB* 61:6.

[141] *Vit.* 414-415, 426-427; cf. *A.J.* 3.276.

[142] 11QT^a/11Q19 63.10-15.

[143] *4QMMT* C 6-7.

[144] *Jub.* 28:16-24.

[145] *Jub.* 36:23-24; cf. also *T. Iss.* 1:2 – 2:5.

[146] Gen 30:14-21.

[147] *QG* 3.21; *Abr.* 253.

[148] Sir 26:5-6; 28:15; 37:11a.

origin,[149] and between Elkanah and Hannah, the mother of Samuel.[150] The issue in both was fertility, but the disputes, as with Rachel and Leah, allow us to see that sexual intercourse was not only about propagation, but also about affection and intimacy. *2 Enoch* tells us that sterility was also an issue for Sothonim, the wife of Nir. She proposed that he therefore take a second wife, only for God to intervene and a miraculous conception take place, leading to the birth of the great priest, Melchizedek.[151] The so-called Babatha documents, an early second century C. E. cache of largely domestic and commercial documents found in caves in the Judean desert, show that Babatha was one of two wives of a certain Judah. After his death she had then to fight her rival over claims and obligations.

Jewish law had provisions for dealing with disputes between children of rival wives in polygynous marriages, giving priority to the firstborn.[152] Both Philo and Josephus address the matter.[153] Philo even refers to polyandry to defend Tamar's virtue, who slept with her father-in-law,[154] but only as an exception. The issue of inheritance rights among children of polygynous marriages appears to have been addressed in the *Temple Scroll*, though the detail, which would have come between the end of column 63 and the beginning of column 64, has not survived. Its discussions of captive women[155] and of levirate marriage[156] assume polygyny, but it prohibits polygyny for the king.[157] Israel's history, not least the story of David and Solomon and their many issues with their wives, provided sufficient rationale for the restriction. The *Damascus Document* then extends that prohibition to all, linking it to greed for wealth, probably through the acquisition of additional dowries.[158] Its argument supporting monogyny cites the creation account that God made humans male and female, and connects it with the story of Noah's ark where the animals entered the ark two by two.[159] It also includes reference to the rule against the king multiplying wives but then exonerates David, in whose time the law was hidden, so not known.[160]

---

[149] *LAB* 42:1-10.

[150] *LAB* 50:1-5.

[151] *2 Enoch* 71:1-2.

[152] Deut 21:15-17.

[153] Philo *Virt.* 115; Josephus *A.J.* 4.249-250.

[154] *Fug.* 153.

[155] 11QT^a/11Q19 63.10-15.

[156] 4QT^b/4Q524.

[157] 11QT^a/11Q19 57.15-19.

[158] CD 4.18.

[159] CD 4.21 – 5.6; Gen 1:27; 7:9.

[160] CD 4.20 – 5.2; cf. Deut 17:17.

While Josephus reflects the widespread view, attested as early as Ben Sira, that Solomon's many wives ruined him,[161] he explains Herod's having nine wives as reflecting Jewish ancestral custom and something to be valued.[162] In the *Jewish War (B.J.)*, he notes that Herod very much liked the custom.[163] His account, however, of Herod is replete with evidence that it could cause chaos.

While polygyny was still in evidence in our period, as reflected in the advice offered about how to handle it, it was increasingly limited to those who could afford it. The book, *Instruction*, whose exposition of the Genesis 2 we encountered in the first chapter, assumes monogyny, probably because it envisages its audience as mainly the poor. Elites like Herod with many wives were an exception. Monogyny is probably assumed as the norm in the *Testaments of the Twelve Patriarchs*,[164] accounting for why the author seems not to reckon with the possibility of Judah's son, Shelah, taking Tamar in levirate marriage.[165]

Inheritance

The matter of producing heirs was of paramount importance. In Abraham's case it related to divine promises about a wonderful future,[166] but for most it simply meant survival. Each new generation cared for the previous generation. It mattered to have children and in such circumstances it mattered especially to have sons. Daughters would be married off to other families, but this was also why choice of the right wife for one's son mattered. The family needed to continue to be productive economically, but also produce the next generation, in turn, as the cycle continued.

Producing offspring was paramount to the extent that for some, as we shall see in chapter 4, it could also define what was sexually deviant as whatever did not aim to procreate. Oftentimes the goal of procreation is very explicit, such as in the angel's instruction in *Pseudo-Philo* to Manoah to go and have sexual intercourse with Eluma,[167] enabling her to give birth to Samson; in the report about ceding Agag the opportunity of one last night of intercourse with his wife before his execution, as a result of which Saul's executioner was conceived;[168] and in the exhortation in *Pseudo-Phocylides* to marry and so pay nature back for its

---

[161] *A.J.* 8.193.

[162] *A.J.* 17.14, 19-23.

[163] *B.J.* 1.477.

[164] *T. Reub.* 4:1; cf. also *T. Iss.* 7:2.

[165] Cf. *T. Jud.* 11:3.

[166] Gen 12:1-3.

[167] *LAB* 42:7.

[168] *LAB* 58:3-4.

generosity with offspring.[169] The author of the *Testaments of the Twelve Patriarchs* makes Rachel into a model of desiring sexual intercourse only for procreation.[170] As we shall see below, not all saw procreation as the sole justification for sex. It remained however always in the foreground as survival and security depended on it, including future inheritance and ensuring control of assets belonged in the family.

Normally only sons inherited, but where a man had only daughters, the law provided for them to marry within the clan with the assumption that their father's inheritance would pass to them and so by marriage to their husband's family.[171] Philo's exposition adds that where their father had given them no dowry, daughters should inherit equally with sons on his death.[172] He then stipulates that the head magistrate should later ensure that they marry within the clan, much as in Tobit.[173] This is different from Greek and Roman law, where normally both sons and daughters could inherit. Foreign influence is probably the reason why in the fifth century B. C. E. Jewish community at Elephantine, both could inherit, as the surviving papyri show.

Concern with offspring accounts for the law according to which a brother should offer to marry his brother's widow, even if it means adding another woman to the household beside his own wife, so-called levirate marriage.[174] She had the right of refusal. Levirate marriage was a primitive form of security for widows, who otherwise could return to their parental household if it still existed or could remarry, usually the best choice. With limited life expectancy, much greater vulnerability to disease and disaster than we can imagine, and with the frequency of death in childbirth, it was not uncommon for people to marry more than once. The Sadducees' mischievous question to Jesus about the woman married seven times to seven brothers and whom she would sleep with in the age to come[175] reflects this provision.

Some marriages would therefore be polygynous as a result of a man, already married, marrying his brother's widow. Increasingly exposure to the subtly attractive values of the fashionable Hellenistic and Roman culture would have undermined the practice, though Greek culture had provisions to ensure that where the sole surviving offspring of a man was a daughter, she be married off to someone within the wider family, so as to retain the inheritance within it. Among some of the values in Greco-Roman culture which Jews could admire was

---

[169] *Ps.-Phoc.* 175-176.

[170] *T. Iss.* 2:3.

[171] Num 27:1-11; 36:8-9; Tob 6:12.

[172] *Spec.* 2.125.

[173] *Spec.* 2.126; similarly *Mos.* 2.234-245; cf. Tob 4:12.

[174] Deut 25:5-10.

[175] Mark 12:18-27.

monogynous marriage, which eventually supplanted polygyny. That brought with it new problems to which we shall return, namely what to do when relationship with one's wife broke down and the option was no longer acceptable to take another.

Incest

Both in Greco-Roman culture and in Jewish culture there were rules which set some limits to a householder's sexual behaviour and applied generally to all within the household. These are provisions about sex with near kin. We noted these restrictions in relation to licit marriage partners. They apply equally within the household, prohibiting sexual relations with daughters, daughters-in-law, granddaughters, and other family members' wives.[176]

There are significant instances of incest within the stories of Genesis. Lot's daughters, confronted by the nightmare of believing that they were earth's sole survivors, or, as they put it, "there is not a man on earth to come to us after the manner of all the world",[177] and concerned to ensure male offspring for their father, made him drunk and slept with him.[178] The story serves racist ideology in explaining the origin of neighbouring peoples, the Moabites and the Ammonites, as descended from the children born to the daughters. Interestingly both Philo and Josephus can show sympathy for the daughters' plight,[179] though Philo can also condemn them in other contexts.[180] *Jubilees* extends moral disapproval to Lot himself.[181]

Jubilees makes a feature of the account preserved in a single verse in Genesis of Reuben, Jacob's eldest, raping Bilhah, Jacob's slave concubine.[182] It forges links with David's sin with Bathsheba by depicting Bilhah as bathing[183] and then depicts her as asleep when the deed occurs. The version in the *Testaments of the Twelve Patriarchs* appears to want to improve the account by claiming she was not only asleep but dead drunk![184] In neither account is there strong focus on the rape as violence done to Bilhah. Rather, it is on incest and on the infringement of Jacob's rights, who from that point must cease engaging sexually with her.[185]

---

[176] Lev 18:6-16; 20:11-12, 17, 19-21; Deut 27:20, 22-23.
[177] Gen 19:31.
[178] Gen 19:30-38.
[179] Philo *QG* 4.56, 58; Josephus *A.J.* 1.204-205.
[180] *Post.* 175-176; *Ebr.* 165-169.
[181] *Jub.* 16:8.
[182] Gen 35:22; cf. 49:5; 1 Chron 5:1; *Jub.* 33:2-9.
[183] 2 Sam 11:2.
[184] *T. Reub.* 3:13.
[185] *Jub.* 33:9; *T. Reub.* 3:15.

Reuben's incestuous deed receives attention in two further documents found among the Dead Sea Scrolls.[186]

Jubilees develops also the third account in Genesis relating to incest, that of Judah's unwitting act of incest with his daughter-in-law, Tamar, who lured him as a prostitute to protest against his inaction in not giving her to Judah's now grown up son after the death of both older brothers.[187] Apart from laying greater blame on Judah's Canaanite wife and so on Judah for marrying a foreigner, who keeps meddling to make things worse, *Jubilees* uses the story as a platform to attack incest, though not without rehabilitating Judah after his repentance and so explaining why he was not executed as Leviticus demands.[188] He was after all the ancestor of the Davidic house. *Jubilees* also makes Tamar a virgin before the encounter with Judah, somewhat ameliorating the offence in the author's eyes.

The story as retold in *Pseudo-Philo* makes Tamar a hero, "our mother", for she chose incest rather than sleeping with foreigners, seen as a much greater evil,[189] a theme already highlighted in *Jubilees*. Philo, too, hails Tamar as virtuous,[190] saying nothing of the incest, and even seeing Judah as a model of the inquiring mind, and even of God.[191] Josephus, by contrast, omits both the incest with Tamar and Reuben's with Bilhah, not nice stories to tell a respectable Roman audience when trying to impress them of Judaism's nobility. On the other hand he includes the rape and incest perpetrated on another Tamar, by Amnon, her brother, as an act of unrestrained passion.[192]

The *Testaments of the Twelve Patriarchs*, for its part, make Judah's incest the major theme of his testamentary speech, as it does Reuben's of his. Following *Jubilees* it makes Bathshua, Judah's Canaanite wife and her meddling interference, the source of all the subsequent troubles, and highlights Judah's error in marrying a foreigner.[193] The author adds alcohol to the story, as he did to the account of Reuben and Bilhah. Accordingly, Judah was drunk when he committed the deed, so had diminished control of his passions and was therefore also not able to recognise Tamar.[194] Little is said explicitly about the incest or Tamar's part in it beyond her being in the category, woman, which according to this author spelled danger to men.

---

[186] 4QcommGen A/4Q252; *4QNarrative A*/4Q458.

[187] Genesis 38; *Jub.* 41:1-21; cf. Lev 18:15; 20:12.

[188] *Jub.* 41:24-25; cf. Lev 18:29.

[189] *LAB* 9:5.

[190] *Fug.* 153; *Leg.* 3.74; *Virt.* 222; *Congr.* 124; *Deus* 137.

[191] *Mut.* 134-136.

[192] *A.J.* 7.162-180; cf. 2 Sam 13:1-22.

[193] *T. Jud.* 10:6; 11:1; *Jub.* 41:7.

[194] *T. Jud.* 12:3.

Incest must have been a problem in our period, because we find it addressed also elsewhere, sometimes in quite general terms. It appears twice among the lists of sins in the *Damascus Document*.[195] Another document is probably referring to incest, when it speaks of someone as "also ... a lover of his near relative".[196] Some write of inappropriate relations with near kin,[197] probably between parents and children,[198] an evil addressed in the *Psalms of Solomon*, a collection of psalms composed in Hebrew in the turbulent middle decades of the first century B. C. E.[199] These are instances from within the Jewish homeland. We also find such references elsewhere.

Thus in its reworking of Leviticus 18 *Pseudo-Phocylides* attacks incest with not only one's mother and stepmother, but also one's father's concubine.[200] Philo contrasts Israel's laws in this regard with the incest which he finds affirmed in other cultures, such as among the Persians,[201] in the story of Oedipus, in the alleged laws of Solon permitting marriage to half-sisters and among the Spartans who permitted marriage even to full sisters.[202]

Love and Marriage

The primary relation between husband and wife was fundamental to the household, although, as Philo reminds us, the household itself had higher priority.[203] The notion of marriage as a private indulgence was foreign. "Love-marriages", as opposed to arranged marriages, were not the norm. At the same time marriage was usually more than utilitarian and minders often succeeded in producing matches which generated love, with or without consulting those involved, although the ideal was to have a coupling which matched attraction already felt. Jacob's marriage to Rachel, Rebecca's to Isaac, and Joseph's to Aseneth, are models of such fulfilment. The last generated the romance, *Joseph and Aseneth*, in which the author seeks to win favour for marriage to proselytes against those who opposed intermarriage with non-Jews, an issue we address in the next chapter.

---

[195] CD 6.14 – 7.4b; 8.3-9.

[196] 4Q477 8.

[197] 4QApocJer C^b/4Q387 fr. A; 4QInstr^d/4Q418 101 ii. 5.

[198] 4QApocrJer A/4Q383 fr. A.

[199] *Pss. Sol.* 8:9-11.

[200] *Ps.-Phoc.* 179-183.

[201] Similarly *Sib. Or.* 7:42-45.

[202] *Spec.* 3.12-28.

[203] *QG* 1.26; *Spec.* 3 170-172.

The oneness in flesh announced in the Genesis myth[204] will have meant more than new kinship for many, but carried with it the sense of union and intimacy which is universally attested where loving engagement thus finds its fulfilment.[205] As we noted in the previous chapter, coming together in sexual union, symbolic of coming together in marriage, was understood as creating something permanent. That was the ideal and probably the reality for most, at least in intention. Marital love comes to expression also in the *Visions of Amram*, when Amram declares his love for Jochabed, explaining that this was the reason why, while away in Canaan, he did not avail himself of the opportunity to take another wife.[206]

Similarly, the *Damascus Document*, otherwise noted for its strong warnings against sexual wrongdoing and legal provisions, clearly affirms marriage as something positive. It includes instruction to ensure the safeguarding of marriages and to deal with matters such as contracting marriages and divorce and how to handle any children involved.[207] *Pseudo-Phocylides* cites Homer's homage to marital bliss.[208] Philo affirms sexual pleasure in the first couple's encounter, despite his constant worries about pleasure's dangers elsewhere.[209] Funeral inscriptions often reflected such love and affection.

Getting married was accordingly a good thing to do. When his enemy Nicanor advises Judas Maccabeus to settle down and marry, the author of 2 Maccabees, who wrote in the late second century B. C. E, in heavy dependence on Jason of Cyrene, whom he in part summarises, clearly views it in a positive light.[210] There are many stories about making sure that people marry. *Pseudo-Philo*, for instance, reports initiatives to find husbands for Kenaz's daughters[211] and for having the Danites find themselves wives.[212] For all its bawdy style, the *Tale of the Three Youths*, assumes marriage as a lifelong partnership[213] and the ideal future was often pictured as one centred around marriage and family life.[214]

We frequently find indirect evidence of how marriage, including the joy of sexual intimacy, was affirmed, above all when it served as an image of hope and bliss. Already in Isaiah we read: "For as a young man marries a young woman, so shall your builder marry you, and as the bridegroom rejoices over the bride, so

---

[204] Gen 2:24.

[205] So Plutarch, *Conj. praec.* 20.

[206] 4Q543 4 2-4 = 4Q544 1 7-9 = 4Q547 1-2 iii.6-9a.

[207] CD 13.17b-19a / 4QD^a/4Q266 9 iii.6-9a.

[208] *Ps.-Phoc.* 195-197.

[209] *Opif.* 151-152.

[210] 2 Macc 14:23.

[211] *LAB* 29:2.

[212] *LAB* 48:3.

[213] 1 Esdr 4:25; echoing Gen 2:24.

[214] So *Sib. Or.* 3:594, 767-795; similarly *T. Abr.* A10:3.

shall your God rejoice over you."[215] Conversely, images of doom refer to absence of such joy, specifically marital. "And I will bring to an end the sound of mirth and gladness, the voice of the bride and bridegroom in the cities of Judah and in the streets of Jerusalem; for the land shall become a waste".[216] The joy of weddings, including sexual pleasure, continued to inspire visions of hope,[217] or their absence, visions of doom.[218]

Wedding imagery functions similarly in early Christian tradition, probably reaching back to Jesus, himself. Mark has him defend his open engagement in celebratory meals with sinners by portraying himself as like a bridegroom and his time, therefore, as like the coming of the groom to his bride.[219] His parable of the great feast[220] was reworked to become a royal invitation to the wedding feast of the king's son.[221] The wedding feast at Cana in John's gospel employs the marital symbolism to convey its message that Jesus brings salvation,[222] echoed later in Jesus' claim to be a bridegroom.[223] Its account of Jesus meeting a Samaritan woman at a well plays intertextually with similar encounters in Genesis and Exodus where suitors court their future spouses.[224]

Marriage, sexual union, and the celebrations which surrounded them were part of normal life to be valued and enjoyed and therefore served well to symbolise hope in a world in which pleasures were few. Wedding feasts were, like the special feasts associated with offering sacrifices, a rare event which lightened up life that for most was hard and in which many would have been hungry. The joy of bride and bridegroom was part of that. Sexual pleasure belonged, as did wine and song.

Despite all the concern about producing offspring, which had patriarchs sleeping with their slaves at their wives' behests, sexual pleasure and sexual intimacy were also valued for themselves. Even Philo, who so often insists on procreation as the sole purpose of sex, cannot bring himself to insist that parents no longer able to fulfil that goal should cease sexual intimacy.[225] His view echoes Plato, who having insisted that sex for procreation be mandatory and the sole function of sexual intercourse during one's fertile years, happily affirms sexual

---

[215] Isa 62:5.

[216] Jer 7:34; similarly 16:9; 25:10; 33:10-11; Joel 2:16.

[217] 4Q434 2 6.

[218] Bar 2:23; *2 Bar.* 10:13-16; 1 Macc 1:27.

[219] Mark 2:19-20; Matt 9:15; Luke 5:34-35; cf. also John 3:29.

[220] Luke 14:7, 15-24.

[221] Matt 22:1-14.

[222] John 2:1-10.

[223] John 3:29.

[224] John 4:1-42; cf. Gen 24:10-61 (Isaac); 29:1-14 (Jacob); Exod 2:15-22 (Moses).

[225] *Spec.* 3.35.

relations after that.[226] Hannah defends her sexual intimacy with Elkanah despite being infertile[227] and Rachel's status as Jacob's lover despite also being infertile affirms such union.[228] At one level was probably the notion that sterile women should just keep trying, but beside this there seems to be acceptance of the role of sexual intercourse as of worth in itself. The values embedded in the myth of oneness through sexual union in Genesis 2 made sense in lived experience.

Conception and Pregnancy

It is important to be aware that the world we are discussing did not have access to safe and reliable contraception, which has transformed modern society in so many ways. It has enabled us more easily to separate in our thinking sex solely for pleasure and affection from sex for propagation. Whether one became pregnant or not then was to a large extent seen as a matter of chance. They had little knowledge of the processes of conception.

There were such things as love potions, as Josephus' stories tell us, including that one was designed to poison Herod.[229] There were also various strategies about fertility enhancement. We read of Rachel and Leah negotiating about their supply.[230] They apparently enabled Leah to conceive again after she had ceased bearing children. The *Testaments of the Twelve Patriarchs* may suggest that Rachel rejected fertility enhancements.[231]

In the book of Wisdom, purporting to be by Solomon, but written in Greek by a well-versed author in the first century C. E., Solomon speaks of conception as resulting from the pleasure of sexual intercourse.[232] Similarly when according to the *Genesis Apocryphon* Lamech is worried that his beautiful son, Noah, may be the fruit of one of the Watchers having slept with his wife, Bitenosh, she reminds him of the pleasure they had experienced in their last sexual intercourse.[233] The assumption is that once she became pregnant they desisted, a value we address in the next chapter, but for the present purpose we note the affirmation of pleasure and its association with conception as in Wisdom.

There appears to have been a view, attested by no less an authority than Hippocrates, that heightened pleasure in sexual intercourse enhanced the chances

---

[226] *Leg.* 784E3-785A3; 783E4-7; 784B1-3.

[227] *LAB* 50:1-5.

[228] Gen 29:30 – 30:24.

[229] *A.J.* 15.223-229; 17.62-64.

[230] Gen 30:14-19.

[231] *T. Iss.* 2:3.

[232] Wis 7:1-2.

[233] 1QapGen ar/1Q20 2.1, 9-10.

of conception occurring,[234] a phenomenon which we now understand as resulting from the additional release of fluids during female orgasm which facilitates the forward movement of sperm. There were two main views of conception itself. Hippocrates understood both men and women to be generating sperm during intercourse, out of which an embryo emerged as male or female depending on the proportions from each partner. This view is reflected in Hebrews, when the author refers to Sarah producing sperm.[235]

The alternative and widely held view, associated with Aristotle, was that the man deposited sperm in the woman, as seed into the soil, where it grew through the nourishment which her blood supplied.[236] Men and women had complementary roles. This complementarity appeared also to be represented in female genitalia, which Galen later explained as an inside-out version of male genitalia.[237]

Some writings reflect a keen interest in the processes. We see this in 4 Ezra which draws on a fairly extensive repertoire of such knowledge for use in analogies. Beyond noting that pregnancies normally lasted nine months and ended in painful contractions in giving birth,[238] it tells us that the first children to be born are stronger, the last, smaller and weaker,[239] an observation better accounted for by likely increased poverty than age or sequence.

Among the collection of poems in the *Thanksgiving Hymns* at Qumran we find references to birth and breastfeeding,[240] even depicting God's love as like the nourishment of a wet nurse.[241] Its use of the images of two pregnant women show keen awareness of the processes of giving birth.[242] In 4 Maccabees the author writes of pregnancies, described as ten months in duration, as a period of formation through the mother's blood and resulting in special bonds between siblings.[243] The work also includes references to childbirth, breastfeeding, and early nurture of children[244] and includes the claim that the more children a woman bears the more she is attached to them.[245]

---

[234] Hippocrates *Genit.* 6.

[235] Heb 11:11.

[236] Aristotle *Gen. an.* 727A29-30.

[237] Galen *UP* 14.6.

[238] 4 Ezra 4:40-42.

[239] 4 Ezra 5:46-52.

[240] 1QHodayot^a/1QH^a xvii.29b-31.

[241] 1QHodayot^a/1QH^a xv.20b-22; xvii.36.

[242] 1QHodayot^a/1QH^a xi.1-18.

[243] 4 Macc 16:7; 13:20-21.

[244] 4 Macc 13:19-22; 15:4-7; 16:6-11; cf. also 2 Macc 7:27; *LAB* 51:2-3.

[245] 4 Macc 15:5.

Pseudo-Philo shows a similar interest in the processes of childbirth,[246] adding reference to women and children where his sources had none.[247] It notes that pregnancy is invisible in the first three months,[248] mentions failed pregnancies and child deaths among the Philistines,[249] and (for no clear reason) declares it blessed to be born from a seven month pregnancy.[250] It describes Moses as like a woman in labour when confronted by Israel's idolatry with the golden calf at Sinai,[251] and uses breastfeeding imagery in relation to Hannah,[252] and Jonathan and David's intimacy.[253] Strikingly it has Deborah declare that earth produced the rib from which Israel was born, emphasising women as life-givers and bypassing Adam.[254]

Philo knew that there was some connection between menstrual blood and the foetus, and wrote of the solidifying of the foetus in the womb after seven days, and the formation of the embryo after 40 or 45 days.[255] For some reason, which my consultations with gynaecologists have left unexplained or, better, confirmed as invalid, he believed eight month pregnancies were dangerous, but seven month ones were not (but blessed according to *LAB*, we noted above).[256] With many others he shared the Aristotle's view that men plant seed and women incubate it.

Just as weddings served as images of joy, so images of conception and birth served as metaphors for new insight ("conception" still does!), labour pain for the process of bringing forth the new, birth for new beginnings (new birth), breastfeeding for learning, and bringing up children for the processes of education. Each metaphorical application is simultaneously by implication an affirmation of the process as a whole or could be. The depiction of pain and sorrow as like the pain of childbirth was a common image. Sometimes it was expanded, as in *1 Enoch*, where the author writes of "a woman in labor, when the child enters the mouth of the womb, and she has difficulty in giving birth".[257] Ben Sira urges his hearers to remember their mother's pain.[258]

The processes of conception and birth could also be a nightmare. Rape, including in marriage, was devastating then as it is now. Pregnancies could be

---

[246] *LAB* 23:4, 7.

[247] *LAB* 5:4-7.

[248] *LAB* 9:5.

[249] *LAB* 55:4, 6, 10.

[250] *LAB* 23:8.

[251] *LAB* 12:5.

[252] *LAB* 51:3.

[253] *LAB* 62:10.

[254] *LAB* 32:15; cf. also Jdt 16:14; Gen 2:22; Ps 104:30.

[255] *QG* 4.27.

[256] *QG* 4.27; *Leg.* 1.9; *Opif.* 124.

[257] *1 Enoch* 62:4.

[258] Sir 7:27-28; similarly Tob 4:3.

unwanted, by one or both parents. Provisions punishing violence which resulted in spontaneous abortions[259] were extrapolated into prohibitions of deliberately procured abortion, for which that world had very crude mean. Jews generally rejected procured abortion and opposed the practice of infanticide, which dumped unwanted babies, especially females, left to be eaten by stray animals. They earned for that a reputation which authors like Hecataeus of Abdera[260] and Tacitus[261] cite as the reasons why Jewish population grew so rapidly.

The third book of the *Sibylline Oracles*, most of which was composed in the second century B. C. E. in Egypt, demands that parents should never abandon their infants but rear and nurture them.[262] It ranks not doing so alongside pederasty and adultery.[263] *Pseudo-Phocylides* attacks abortion.[264] The *Epistle of Enoch*, the fifth main section of *1 Enoch*,[265] dating probably from the mid second century B. C. E, fears a future where parents will sell their babies and procure abortions.[266] The *Parables of Enoch* blames the Watcher, Kasdeya, for teaching techniques to induce abortions.[267] The techniques of abortion typically employed the use of herbs or direct physical intervention. Philo similarly condemns abortion[268] and links the practice of child exposure to obsession with self-indulgent sex,[269] for which parents should hide their faces in shame.[270]

Constantly becoming pregnant, going through the pain of childbirth, and then repeating the process over and over again, was exhausting and debilitating for many, who well knew the truth of Gen 3:16 which predicted such pain and were forced for their salvation, their security, to subject themselves to their husbands and the demands of his household, as the author of 1 Timothy suggests, which we noted in chapter 1.[271] Average life expectancy across the Roman empire in our period was around 25-30. Half the women who reached 15 years of age were dead before their mid to late thirties, many dying in childbirth. It is estimated that fewer than half the children born survived.

---

[259] Exod 21:22-23.
[260] Diodorus 40.3.8.
[261] Tacitus *Hist.* 5.5.3.
[262] *Sib. Or.* 3:765-766; see also 5:145-146.
[263] *Sib. Or.* 3:764.
[264] *Ps.-Phoc.* 184-186.
[265] *1 Enoch* 92 – 105.
[266] *1 Enoch* 99:5.
[267] *1 Enoch* 69:12.
[268] Philo *Hypoth.* 7.7.
[269] *Spec.* 3.110-119.
[270] *Virt.* 131-133.
[271] 1 Tim 2:14-15.

It is interesting that some writings add to women's pain predicted in Gen 3:16, the pain of bringing up of children,[272] which was their task in the early years before the child, at least the male one, became old enough to be instructed by his father, or his father's slave. That stage is assumed in the instructions in Colossians and Ephesians which depict upbringing of children as the father's role.[273]

Public Affairs of the Household

Affairs connecting the household with the wider world were in the hands of its master. Households significant enough to engage in commerce and similar connections would usually have public space on the street side of the house where access was relatively free for people to come and go, and meals or feasts might take place which could be observed by passers by. Some of the meals of Jesus in with doubtful companions assume this,[274] as do mission instructions about entering others' houses.[275] Commerce was male business and meals might be male only. Depending on the company and the values, they might be occasions of sophisticated exchange and entertainment, such as listening to a wandering philosopher or a teacher like Jesus.

Entertainment might extend however to more bawdy pursuits with dancing girls, musicians, and local prostitutes. The "sinners" in the anecdotes about Jesus' attendance at such meals may well have included some or all of the above. In their grossest form such parties became orgies of sexual excess, where drunkenness and promiscuity combined, with indiscriminate sexual indulgence going on with whomever was available, female or male. Philo rails against such occasions,[276] as did Jews generally, though some clearly found it an attractive fashion. Wives were usually not present on such occasions. While somewhat more constrained, Antipas' birthday party took place in one room in the palace while his wife and presumably the other respected women were in another location.[277] The exception, as usual, was the entertainment, which might include women, in this case his new stepdaughter, whose dancing won his heart. To consult her mother on what to ask the doting Antipas, she accordingly had to leave the room to find her for advice.

Wives might not have been present at many such gatherings, but remained in private quarters. This did not mean they were cloistered in seclusion on a daily basis. Many would walk to the market to obtain food and other necessities. Women of poorer means would in any case have nowhere to hide. Modesty

---

[272] 4 Macc 16:8; Philo *Opif.* 167.

[273] Col 3:21; Eph 6:4.

[274] E.g. Mark 2:15-17.

[275] Mark 6:10; Luke 10:5.

[276] *Opif.* 158; *Spec.* 1.192-193; see also *QG* 2.12; *Somn.* 2.147; *Mos.* 2.185.

[277] Mark 6:24.

required they be veiled, much as still in some cultures today. Paul is appalled to hear that some thought worship meant they could abandon their veils, as in Corinth.[278] Being affirmed as equally of worth in God's eyes and in the church did not mean ceasing to be woman or abandoning "normal" and "natural" behaviour. Paul saw the veil not as cultural trapping but as part of the divine order.

Adultery and Forbidden Liaisons

Married perhaps as young as twelve years of age at the extreme and many children later, a woman might have found herself in only her late twenties, while her husband was heading towards fifty. Given low life expectancy and exposure to danger and disease, he might have been on his last legs and she, in full sexual maturity; or she may have been worn out or have died in giving birth to the last child and he, left to begin again. All manner of possibilities emerge. She might find a man who finds her attractive. He would normally remarry. His new wife might be younger than one or more of his sons. The scene is set for one of them to find the new wife especially attractive, the scenario which Paul's warning to Corinth presupposes: a man sleeping with his father's wife.[279]

The ten commandments single out adultery for prohibition.[280] No one really argued against it. It was a shared value across Jewish and non-Jewish cultures of the day. But many acted against it. In a culture where women belonged to men, first to their fathers and then by marriage to their husbands, adultery from a male perspective was taking what belonged to another. It was theft. The perspective of ownership is evident in the tenth commandment which forbids coveting the wife of one's neighbour – alongside coveting his other possessions like "his field, male or female slave, or ox, or donkey".[281]

It was much more than that, however. In an age of uncertain contraception, or none at all, adultery risked that the woman could become pregnant with the adulterer's child. This could be a disaster for a household, its future stability and so its ability to sustain all who depended on it, including both the immediate and the wider family. If it became known, it would bring shame on the perpetrator, but also his family. It would also bring shame on the woman's family, where her husband would be reduced to being a victim, also a matter of shame.

Rarely do we find reference to the impact on the wife of the perpetrator in these male-oriented discussions. The closest we come to this is in Ben Sira who described the adulterer as sinning against his own bed,[282] where he presumably

---

[278] 1 Cor 11:2-16.

[279] 1 Cor 5:1.

[280] Exod 20:14; Deut 5:18; cf. also Lev 20:10; Deut 22:22.

[281] Deut 5:21.

[282] Sir 23:18.

envisages her presence! He also insists that a man keep himself exclusively for his wife, deploring liaisons by either party,[283] a view reiterated in Josephus.[284] The *Testament of the Twelve Patriarchs* hail Isacchar as one who preserved fidelity all his life.[285]

Mostly the focus is on male interests, reflecting the dominant values of the day. One should also not overlook the hurt experienced as a result of such actions. It was rarely articulated, but doubtless widely felt. Ben Sira probably includes it when he speaks of the "wounds of the heart".[286]

In common to both Jewish and non-Jewish cultures was the requirement that a woman who had engaged in adultery be dismissed from the marriage, that is, divorced. The emperor Augustus reasserted this requirement over against a tendency not to carry this through consistently in Roman society and ruled that the husband must prosecute the offender within 60 days.[287] Fathers could kill both if caught in the act and the husband could kill the male perpetrator if he belonged to a lower class. Otherwise, both perpetrators were to be banished to different islands. Greek family law also demanded divorce for adultery. Such provisions are understandable given the possibilities then of pregnancy and the havoc that could produce.

Jewish law demanded the death penalty for both.[288] While both Philo[289] and Josephus[290] boasted of the Law's strictness in imposing such a sentence, in reality, as that became no longer possible when Jews lost the right to execute capital punishment, the woman had at least to become effectively dead for the man through divorce and he must never receive her back, not even in the far off future. Josephus mentions that the first husband of Herod's sister, Salome, had been executed for adultery,[291] and that Herod executed Mariamme and his uncle for adultery,[292] but these were atypical executions performed under regal prerogative. The test case with which Jesus was confronted in the floating tradition about the woman taken in adultery, preserved by most manuscripts in John 7:53 - 8:11 reflects the dilemma: the Jewish Law required execution but Roman Law forbad it. What would Jesus do?

---

[283] Sir 36:24-27; 23:18-26.

[284] *Ap.* 2.201.

[285] *T. Iss.* 7:2.

[286] Sir 25:13.

[287] *Lex Iulia de maritandis ordinibus* 18 B. C. E., updated in *Lex Papia Poppaea* 9 C. E.

[288] Lev 20:10; Deut 22:22; Prov 2:16-19; 7:25-27; assumed also in Sir 9:9; Sus 22.

[289] Philo *Spec.* 3.11; *Hypoth.* 7:1.

[290] *A.J.* 3.274-275; 7.130-131; *Ap.* 2.215.

[291] *B.J.* 1.486.

[292] *B.J.* 1.443.

Cases in dispute of alleged adultery were regulated according to the rite of bitter waters.[293] Blatant or exposed adultery demanded divorce. Underlying that was also the belief that sleeping with another rendered one unclean to return to the original partner. The provision in Deut 24:1-4, one of the rare though incidental references to divorce, also makes that clear.

Similarly, sexual intercourse between a betrothed woman and someone other than her betrothed originally demanded the death penalty for both involved,[294] but with the disappearance of the possibility of the death penalty, divorce was mandated. Accordingly, Joseph assumes he must divorce Mary, whom he suspects of the equivalent of adultery,[295] namely engaging in intercourse with someone other than her betrothed. Such behaviour may well be being addressed in one passage in the *Damascus Document*,[296] if it is not referring to chastity of widows.

There is no shortage of expositions of the prohibition of adultery. Many focus on the destructive impact on households. Ben Sira deplores the secrecy and deceit which adultery entailed,[297] a feature noted of adulterous predators in the Psalms of Solomon[298] and Susanna, and whether on the part of men or women.[299] According to Ben Sira the adulteress spurns God's Law, wrongs her husband, and brings illegitimate children into the household.[300] He is equally harsh in criticising predatory old men.[301] In keeping with his pessimism he fears the unmarried man, because, he alleges, he is likely to raid others' plots.[302] As noted earlier, Ben Sira goes beyond the notion that adultery is theft of what belongs to another man to assert that it is also an act which wrongs one's wife.[303]

The Wisdom of Solomon focuses on the detrimental effects of adultery on households and their security, predicting that in the judgement the offspring will lay charges against their parents.[304] Wisdom makes adultery typically a behaviour associated with idolaters,[305] a connection alleged also in Book 3 of the *Sibylline Oracles*.[306]

---

[293] Num 5:13-31; cf. also 4QD^e/4Q270 4 1-8.

[294] Deut 22:23-24.

[295] Matt 1:18-19.

[296] 4QD^e/4Q270 2 i.17.

[297] Sir 23:18-21.

[298] *Pss. Sol.* 4

[299] Sir 23:22-26.

[300] Sir 23:23.

[301] Sir 25:2; 42:8.

[302] Sir 36:30-31.

[303] Sir 23:18.

[304] Wis 3:12, 16-18; 4:3-6.

[305] Wis 14:24-26.

[306] *Sib. Or.* 3:36-38, 594-595, 764; similarly 4:31-34; 5:430; 1:178.

Being born of illicit sexual relations, a so-called *mamzer*, was deemed a matter of shame, oddly reflected in the coarse appellation, "bastard!", still today, since no one so born can be deemed responsible for how they came into the world. The author of Book 3 of the *Sibylline Oracles* makes such allegations against Alexander the Great,[307] and others did so against John Hyrcanus[308] and by implication also against his son, Alexander Janneus.[309] The *Psalms of Solomon* graphically describe how a male predator could slink his way into households and wreck them with adultery.[310] The author allies him with Eden's snake as a seducer, a reading Greek Genesis made possible.[311]

The author of *Pseudo-Philo* introduces adultery as the first major sin with which people brought defilement on themselves,[312] treats worshippers of the golden calf at Sinai like adulterers making them drink bitter water,[313] and highlights it as a sin linked with the tribe of Gad.[314] It connects the prohibition against adultery with the prohibition of lusting after a neighbour's wife,[315] as do the author of 4 Maccabees[316] and *Pseudo-Philemon*.

Philo singles out adultery as the greatest of all crimes,[317] which he sees symbolised in its taking first place in the second table of the ten commandments, at least as preserved in the Greek translation, whereas in the Hebrew this is not so. This order is reflected also in *Pseudo-Phocylides*,[318] *Pseudo-Philo*,[319] and in many New Testament texts.[320] Philo singles out three groups of people affected by adultery: the family of the man against whom the adultery is committed (by someone sleeping with his wife); the family and friends of the male perpetrator, because it brings shame on them; the children of the marriage who face an uncertain future.[321] He also makes it the umbrella under which to discuss all other acts of sexual wrongdoing.

---

[307] *Sib. Or.* 3:381-387.
[308] *T. Mos.* 5:4; cf. Josephus *A.J.* 13.292.
[309] *A.J.* 13.373.
[310] *Ps. Sol.* 4:20; similarly 15:11.
[311] *Ps. Sol.* 4:9-10.
[312] *LAB* 2:8-10.
[313] *LAB* 12:7.
[314] *LAB* 25:10.
[315] *LAB* 44:6-7.
[316] 4 Macc 2:4-6.
[317] *Ios.* 42-44.
[318] *Ps.-Phoc.* 3-8.
[319] *LAB* 11:10.
[320] Luke 18:20-21; Mark 7:21; 1 Cor 6:9.
[321] Philo *Decal.* 126-131.

In a number of texts Joseph is hailed as the model in resisting adultery with his master's wife.[322] In the romance, *Joseph and Aseneth*, he must do so, over against not just his master's wife, but all the women of Egypt who were forever wanting to seduce him.[323] The *Testaments of the Twelve Patriarchs* similarly praises Joseph,[324] having earlier given special attention to the nature of the temptation. In this it blames women as unable to control their passions and deliberately going about to seduce men, as their forebears had done to the Watchers.[325] Blaming women was widespread, but in most texts men who responded to such women are portrayed as weak and stupid. Holofernes fell for Judith's would-be seduction and met his end,[326] as had Sisera to Jael's earlier.[327] *Jubilees* is noteworthy in its version of the Watcher myth for not laying any blame on the women involved.

Jesus' exposition of the prohibition in Matt 5:28 shifts the focus from act to attitude. In doing so it appears to connect the prohibition of adultery with the 10th commandment, coveting/lusting after what belongs to someone else. This connection appears elsewhere in Jewish literature.[328] In the particular twist given by Jesus the man is made responsible, not just for any act of adultery, but already for adulterous desire.[329] The text has been misread as referring to a man looking at any woman and to any sexual response to women. Its effect would be to condemn all sexual responses to women as adulterous, with the disastrous effect of depicting all women as dangerous and in need of covering and strict control by men.

Instead the text, in dealing with adultery, is speaking about married women. It then argues that any man who looks at a married woman with a view to wanting to have sex with her, has committed adultery with her already in his heart. It puts the responsibility back on the man to control what he does, not only in action but also in attitude and with his sexual responses. Indirect confirmation of this as likely to represent his stance is his lack of compunction about having women in his company as he journeyed around Galilee and up to Jerusalem. Nowhere in that context do we read of their being treated as dangerous or a threat. That includes his response to the informal approach by a woman, told in four variations, who wanted to anoint his feet (or head) with oil, causing the men present to recoil in disapproval.[330] His response was not distancing but acceptance. His was in that

---

[322] 1 Macc 2:53-54; *LAB* 43:5; Sus 13; Wis 10:13; 4 Macc 2:2-3; Philo *Ios.* 40-44; Josephus *A.J.* 2.41-60.

[323] *Asen.* 7:3.

[324] *T. Jos.* 3:1 – 9:5.

[325] *T. Reub.* 3:1 – 9:5.

[326] Jdt 13:6-10.

[327] Judg 4:21.

[328] *LAB* 44:6-7, 10; 4 Macc 2:4-6; and Pseudo-Philemon.

[329] Matt 5:28.

[330] Mark 14:3-9; Matt 26:6-13; John 12:1-8; Luke 7:36-50.

sense an open kind of Judaism. The focus on inward attitude and not just action was characteristic of his approach.[331]

Adultery and Divorce

As already mentioned, adultery required divorce. This was not only the widespread assumption, which made sense given the practicalities of pregnancy. It was also the law in Greek, Roman, and Jewish society. In a number of stories we see it playing itself out. We have already mentioned the case of Joseph and Mary where it is assumed.[332] In similar circumstances the priest Nir knows he must divorce his wife Sothonim, pregnant with the fabled Melchizedek, only to learn that this is a divine miracle. *Jubilees* notes that Jacob had to cease sexual relations with Bilhah after another had slept with her, namely Reuben, his son.[333] For the same reason by sleeping with his father, David's, concubines Absalom made it impossible for David ever to sleep with them again.[334] Abner had done the same with Saul's concubine.[335] Josephus sees something similar occurring when Herod's son, Alexander, had sexual relations with Herod's eunuchs.[336]

The concern looms large in the many retellings of Sarah's abduction by Pharaoh, which make every effort to assure hearers that no sexual intercourse took place, since, as they knew, then Abraham should never have taken her back. For not only adultery, but any sexual union with another severed the original union. Thus *Genesis Apocryphon* reports that Abraham prayed that Pharaoh not defile Sarah,[337] even though she had been forcefully abducted.[338] Its story ends with Pharaoh returning Sarah and declaring that he had not "known" or defiled her, that is, had not had sexual intercourse with her.[339] The same concern is evident in *Pseudo-Eupolemus* and in Philo,[340] who makes the point explicitly that Sarah's defilement would have ended the marriage and, as he puts it, the promise of a people dearest to God with priest and prophet would have come to naught.[341] In one of his versions Josephus has God intervene just at the point where Pharaoh

---

[331] See Mark 7:21-23.

[332] Matt 1:18-19.

[333] *Jub.* 33:9; cf. Gen 35:22; similarly *T. Reub.* 3:15.

[334] 2 Sam 20:3; Josephus *A.J.* 7.213-214.

[335] 2 Sam 3:6-12; Josephus *A.J.* 7.23.

[336] Josephus *A.J.* 16.229-234; *B.J.* 1.488-492.

[337] 1QapGen ar/1Q20 20.15.

[338] 1QapGen ar/1Q20 20:14; similarly *Jub.* 13:11, 13.

[339] 1QapGen ar/1Q20 20.30.

[340] *Abr.* 98; *QG* 4.63, 66-67.

[341] *Abr.* 98.

was about to rape Sarah,[342] and in another limits her stay to a single night after which she was "sent back immaculate".[343]

There are some rare exceptions to the rule of never receiving back a woman who had sex with another man and these relate to captive women. In some marriage contracts from the Judean desert we find the stipulation that men were allowed to accept the return of wives taken prisoner, despite the likelihood in many cases that they had been raped.[344] Apart from that Josephus reports actions which assume recall of wives: of Michal to David[345] and Doris to Herod.[346]

When Matthew's versions of Jesus' prohibition of divorce stipulate an exception, "except for adultery", he is giving expression to what all would have assumed was a general rule – as well as being law. This could be an innovation on the part of Matthew or his community to accommodate Jesus' absolute prohibition to what were otherwise the strictest norms of the day, as is often assumed. Then he would be unlocking part of what Jesus had locked in, namely that there is no way out of a marriage that has gone wrong. It is permanent.

The argument used for its permanence derives from the Genesis creation stories we considered in the previous chapter. According to the account preserved in Mark, Jesus responded to a question about the legitimacy of divorce by citing Gen 1:27 about God making humankind male and female and then Gen 2:24, "For this reason a man shall leave his father and mother and be joined to his wife and the two shall become one flesh", adding, "so they are no longer two but one flesh".[347] This led to the declaration: "What therefore God has yoked together, let no human being separate/divorce".[348] The prohibition appears absolute. Human beings should not undo what God has done by joining a man and woman permanently in marriage.

Paul, as we saw, employs Gen 2:24 similarly to argue that a permanent relationship is formed when a person engages in sex with a prostitute. He does so because he argues that the new permanent union severs any previous joining, which he uses to depict the Christian's relation to Christ.[349] Joining with a prostitute separates you from Christ. Thus Gen 2:24 cuts both ways: sex joins and simultaneously severs previous unions. That will be how Matthew will have understood it. I think it likely that the same logic is assumed but not expressed in the anecdote in Mark. The argument about permanence based on Gen 2:24 is

---

[342] *A.J.* 1.161-165.

[343] *B.J.* 5.380-381.

[344] *P. Mur.* 20 and *P. Yadin* 10 = 5/6Hev 10.

[345] *A.J.* 7.25-26.

[346] *B.J.* 1.432; *A.J.* 16.85.

[347] Mark 10:6-8.

[348] Mark 10:9.

[349] 1 Cor 6:16.

implicitly an argument for severance. Matthew then simply spells out what was already implied: adultery severs and so divorce is not just an option; what is more, it is mandated. This seems more credible than that Matthew, noted for insisting on fulfilment of the Law and of Jesus' teachings, had here watered them down. This seems all the more credible when one takes into account that shortly after using Gen 2:24 in this way to argue severance Paul cites the prohibition of divorce.[350] This shows that he could contemplate both notions and so probably also assume that like Matthew it applied to the situation of divorce.

Beside the anecdote, appended to it in Mark and incorporated within it in Matthew's revision, is a saying prohibiting divorce and remarriage as adultery. As it appears in Mark it applies to both a man and a woman: "Whoever divorces his wife and marries another commits adultery against her; and if she divorces her husband and marries another, she commits adultery".[351] Remarriage entails adultery on the basis that the original marriage is still intact and cannot be dissolved. "Against her" is not usually what one might have expected, because adultery was normally seen as something committed against another man. Whether stemming from Jesus or creative tradition, the notion that one can also commit adultery against one's wife puts the saying in line with the thought of Ben Sira, according to whom adultery is also against one's own bed, one's own marriage and wife.[352] The second part, addressing the action of a woman in divorcing her husband, would be unusual, but not unthinkable in a Greco-Roman context, where such divorce was usually through abandoning the husband, such as in the case of divorces in the first century C. E. by Herodias, Drusilla, Berenice, and Mariamme, to which Josephus refers.[353]

How unusual it would have been in a Jewish context is debated. Rabbinic teaching stipulated that only a man could divorce, but some evidence suggests that at an earlier period women could also do so, or, at the very least, take such an initiative. In Josephus we have reference to Salome, Herod's sister, divorcing her husband, Costobarus. She "sent him a document dissolving their marriage", an act of which Josephus (and Herod) strongly disapproved as something which they saw as the preserve of men.[354] Issuing a certificate of divorce, which freed people to remarry, was a distinctively Jewish practice.[355]

Paul assumes that both can divorce.[356] He knows of Jesus' prohibition of divorce and urges reconciliation of those who have divorced or that those divorced

---

[350] 1 Cor 7:10-11.

[351] Mark 10:11-12.

[352] Sir 23:18.

[353] *A.J.* 18.136; *A.J.* 20.143-144; *A.J.* 20.147.

[354] *A.J.* 15.259-260.

[355] Deut 24:1, Isa 50:1, and Jer 3:8 (though not in Hos 2:4).

[356] 1 Cor 7:10-11.

otherwise remain single. This may reflect his preference for singleness anyway, but it could also reflect the prohibition of remarriage, though he does not depict it as adultery.

Jesus' prohibition of divorce appears in different forms in Matthew and Luke, where it probably derives ultimately from their common source.[357] Luke's version sits within teaching directed against greed, so may well be functioning in part as an illustration of greed: divorce in order to remarry for a bigger dowry. It contains the prohibition addressed to the man: "Anyone who divorces his wife and marries another commits adultery", but then adds: "and whoever marries a woman divorced from her husband commits adultery".[358] This also assumes that original marriages are indissoluble, so any new marriage must be an act of adultery. It is possible to translate the second half as: "and whoever marries a woman who has divorced from her husband commits adultery", in which case it, too, like Mark 10:12 would address a woman's taking the initiative.

Matthew brings two versions. Both are set in contrast to Deut 24:1-4, which assumes the legality of divorce. In 5:32 Matthew reports Jesus as saying: "anyone who divorces his wife, except on the ground of unchastity, causes her to commit adultery; and whoever marries a divorced woman commits adultery". Again it is possible to read "divorced woman" as "a woman who has divorced", as in Luke 16:18. The claim that a man divorcing his wife makes her commit adultery assumes that her only real option would be to remarry and since the original marriage was indissoluble she would be committing adultery. It shows some concern for the woman, but at the level of wronging her because of making her sin. The uniqueness of Matthew's version of the saying both here and in his rewriting of Mark 10 is that he includes an exception clause, "except for unchastity". The word translated "unchastity" could simply describe any kind of shameful sexual wrongdoing, as in the ground for divorce in Deut 24:1, taking it in a narrow sense, but it is clear that Matthew has Jesus challenge the ruling in Deut 24:1 by making it stricter. It is fairly obvious that he means adultery and is spelling out what everyone knew was the rule. Adultery required divorce because it destroyed the original relationship and created a new one. While some see Matthew modifying Jesus' absolute stance to fit the normal rule, I have become convinced, rather, that he is simply spelling out what was assumed from the beginning.

Whether Jesus used the Genesis texts in this way or they were cited in support of his general prohibition by those who passed on his teachings, the effect is to portray a very strict, indeed, restrictive attitude. It is not unlikely that divorce was an issue in dispute in his day. If, as it seems, he was closely connected with John

---

[357] Matt 5:32; Luke 16:18; cf. Matt 19:9.

[358] Luke 16:18.

the Baptist, then he will probably have shared John's disapproval of Antipas'
marriage, for breaching the prohibition of marrying one's brother's wife,[359] even
though in this instance she was divorced and he was only a half-brother. Such a
marriage would not be seen as illegal in contemporary marriage law in most legal
jurisdictions today. He may well have, in addition, objected to the blatant
manoeuvring undertaken by Antipas to set up his new marriage which included
arranging convenient divorces to suit his ends. On that we can only speculate.

The shift away from polygyny is also likely to have exacerbated the problem of
divorce. Divorce had always been an option, normally exercised by men, and in
Jewish law entailed giving the woman a certificate of divorce which clearly stated
her release from the marriage and therefore freedom to marry another. In a
polygynous marriage the common practice was simply to take another wife when
trouble occurred with the first wife, short of adultery. With the trend towards
monogynous marriages, divorce would have been the only option if one felt that
staying married was unbearable. That would have raised the issue of the extent to
which a man, in particular, could just arbitrarily make such a decision and on what
grounds.

There are indications of strong disapproval of men who became entrepreneurial
in pursuing new marriages and bigger dowries. In warning against multiple
marriage *Pseudo-Phocylides* probably has this in mind.[360] Ben Sira commends
divorcing a recalcitrant wife,[361] and cautions against marrying a woman with a rich
dowry, where divorce could mean substantial loss.[362] As we have seen, Luke may
well have greed in mind when he incorporates Jesus' prohibition of divorce and
remarriage within a context dealing with avarice.[363]

Women were also criticised for multiple marriages, most notably those who
could act independently like Cleopatra,[364] and Glaphyra.[365] The alternative ideal
was the woman who after divorce or as a widow remained unmarried, called in
Latin *univirae*. Luke's image of Anna the prophetess who remained unmarried[366]
might be appealing to this ideal. Similarly Josephus hails Antonia, widow of
Tiberius' brother Drusus, who never remarried.[367]

Some identify the beginnings of dissatisfaction with the practice of divorce in
Malachi, where it appears that Gen 2:24 has also played a role in arguing for

---

[359] Mark 6:18.
[360] *Ps.-Phoc.* 205-206.
[361] Sir 25:26.
[362] Cf. Sir 25:21; similarly *Ps.-Phoc.* 199-200.
[363] Luke 16:18 in Luke 16:13-31.
[364] *Sib. Or.* 3:357-358.
[365] *A.J.* 17.349-353; *B.J.* 2.114-116.
[366] Luke 2:37.
[367] *A.J.* 18.180.

permanence and against abuse, especially if we read Mal 2:15 as: "has he not made one, which had flesh and spirit"? The text is extremely difficult to interpret, alternatives including that it refers to God hating divorce, or to a man hating (divorcing) his wife. Interestingly, a variant form of the text actually has it affirm the practice of divorce.[368] Tobit's notion of divinely determined marriage partners, a romantic idea which still has wide currency, implies permanence and no divorce,[369] but then as now it probably sat alongside an acceptance of divorce.

Before the full publication of the scrolls many read the *Damascus Document* as prohibiting divorce and remarriage, especially because it speaks of marrying two women in their lifetime.[370] It was hailed as a forerunner of Jesus' teaching on divorce. However the publication of previously unknown fragments of the document found in the Dead Sea caves showed that divorce was presupposed as part of community life and that would have included the permission of the divorced person to remarry.[371] Thus divorce was assumed as part of normal life by the author of the *Temple Scroll*[372] and by the author of the *Damascus Document*. While the latter rejected marriage to women divorced for adultery,[373] it was open to marriage to other divorcees, such as, we imagine, a woman, whose husband had been expelled from the community for lodging an invalid complaint against his wife, since it assumes the presence of divorced women.[374]

Later rabbinic tradition reports that dispute over the matter reached as far back as the first century B. C. E. Evaluating the historicity of such claims is fraught with difficulty, but it is certainly thinkable that the issues would have been discussed, including the two main options canvassed in the tradition: a liberal stance leaving it up to the man who might cite a wide range of misdemeanours, the Pharisaic option associated with Hillel and Akiba[375] and similarly argued by Josephus;[376] and a more conservative one: serious sexual misconduct, the Sadducean option, associated with Shammai.[377] This assumes that both would have agreed that adultery was an automatic ground and mandated divorce.

Whether or not this reflects first century history or later reconstruction, the probability of dispute over divorce in the Jewish context of Jesus is likely. Jesus' stance is then to be understood as a reaction against those advocating divorce,

---

[368] 4QMinor Prophets^a/4Q76.

[369] Tob 6:18; 7:11 GI; 6:13; 7:11; 8:21 GII.

[370] CD 4.20-21.

[371] CD 13.17b-19a / 4QD^a/4Q266 9 iii.6-9a.

[372] 11QT^a/11Q19 66.8-11; cf. also 4Q159/4QOrd^a 2-4+8 8-10; 11QT^a/11Q19 54.4

[373] 4QD^f/4Q271 3.

[374] 4QOrd^a/4Q159; 4QD^a/4Q266 9 iii.5; CD 13.16-17.

[375] *m. Git* 9.10; *b. Git* 90a.

[376] *A.J.* 4.253.

[377] *m. Git* 9.10.

rather than as an engagement in the discussion. His response is somewhat odd, because it not only forbids divorce, and describes remarriage as adultery (because the original marriage still exists), but charges a man who thus remarries with committing adultery, something usually seen as a sin against another man, not a woman. To depict it as something, by implication, committed against a woman (as the version in Mark spells out) is a creative twist. Mark may be responsible for the matching saying about a woman divorcing a man and remarrying. The saying, "What God has joined together, let no human being separate/divorce",[378] takes a form typical in anecdotes about Jesus[379] and may well be authentic. It is a provocation, like most of the other twofold quips found in these stories.

While Jesus' response could well have protected some women from arbitrary dismissal and have men putting more effort into making marriages work, it was hardly adequate to be treated as rule for all occasions. Taken as such it could trap people in abusive and destructive marriages. Similarly prohibiting remarriage would in many instances close off the most realistic and compassionate option for those dismissed, especially where family of origin was no longer an available refuge for women. A divorced woman was left in a very vulnerable position, her hope being: acceptance back into her father's family, but that would be far from assured if he disowned her; remarriage, the safest option; or eking out survival through prostitution.

When Paul confronts divorce at Corinth he urges partners to return to their marriages or remain single.[380] Informing his comments was his general preference for people not to marry, but he seems to have taken prohibition of remarriage as a rule. By contrast, he loosens up the options in applying the prohibition to believers married to unbelievers. They, too, should keep in their marriages, but should accept dissolution of their marriages if the unbelieving partners want it.[381] He appears then to accept that, in accordance with normal Jewish law, they would be free to remarry.

Beside the complex social context which governed sexual values were also those related to matters of cult and ritual purity and to these we turn in the chapter which follows.

---

[378] Mark 10:9.
[379] Cf. Mark 2:9; 2:17a; 2:27; 7:15.
[380] 1 Cor 7:10-11.
[381] 1 Cor 7:12-16.

Sacred Space

At least until its destruction in 70 C. E. the Jerusalem temple was the sacred space for all Jews. It was a place of pilgrimage especially for male Jews and a site for celebration and sacrifice. Stunningly impressive according to all accounts, the temple, renovated and refurbished by Herod, like its predecessors embodied a series of concentric zones of holiness, beginning with the most holy inner sanctum, reaching out to the holy place where priests performed sacrifices, to the court of men, the court of women, the separation of the two an innovation, and the huge outer court, which Gentiles could enter. Holy places were special places where access was necessarily restricted. No one was to enter the temple in a state of impurity. Nearby were many ritual baths or pools where worshippers could immerse to ensure their fitness to enter holy space.

Dealing with Impurity

Being impure at times was part of being human. It was not a matter of sin or guilt, let alone of unworthiness. Women menstruating were for its duration in a state of impurity or uncleanness,[1] as they were also after childbirth, for a week after birth of a boy and two weeks after birth of a girl.[2] They then had a lesser level of impurity banning them from touching holy things or entering the temple for 40 days after birth of a boy, and 80 days after birth of a girl, after which they had to offer sacrifices.[3] Luke is careful to note that Mary observed such provisions after the birth of Jesus,[4] probably reflecting a distinctive Jewish interpretation which

---

[1] Lev 15:19-24.
[2] Lev 12:2, 4.
[3] Lev 12:3, 5-8.
[4] Luke 2:22-24, 27, 39.

went beyond the biblical text in deeming not just the mother, but also the child as in need of purification. The greater length of time after the birth of girls may well reflect the belief that women were more often exposed by natural processes to being unclean.

Men, too, became unclean; thus after ejaculation of semen, whether during sexual intercourse, during sleep, or through masturbation, a topic untouched, but an event to be assumed among most men of the time.[5] After intercourse both the man and the woman were in a state of impurity and needed to bathe in water and would not be deemed pure again until sundown.[6]

Neither the flow of menstrual blood nor the flow of semen represented something bad or evil. It was simply part of life. When it occurred you needed to know what to do. To return to purity or cleanness required time. It also required some ritual like immersion or sprinkling with holy water.

Jewish beliefs about purity and purification were no oddity in the ancient world. On a second century B. C. E. inscription found at the temple of Isis, Sarapis, and Anoubis in Megalopolis in Greece we read of similar purification requirements before entry. The fourth century B. C. E. Greek historian, Herodotus tells that it was standard practice that Greeks and Egyptians never entered temples without first purifying themselves after seminal emission.[7]

Uncleanness was not confined to the broadly sexual dimensions of being human. People became unclean by touching a corpse, which on occasion they would need to do. Such uncleanness required a seven day purification period, which included sprinkling with water mixed with the ashes of a red cow on the first, third, and seventh day.[8] A person in a state of impurity had to take care not to spread that impurity to others or to other things. Sometimes that was unavoidable, such as when a house became unclean as a result of a death. People needed to take care. By following the right steps and letting time pass everything would return to normal.

The abundance of stone water jars, which were considered the best way to keep water ritually pure, and the number of immersion pools found at Jewish settlement sites in both Judea and Galilee, attest to the seriousness with which such purity provisions were observed, and not only those relating broadly to sexuality. They might serve myriad purification functions, such as the six stone jars at the wedding feast in Cana,[9] which were probably used at least for ritual purification of hands before eating. Regular washings first thing in the morning, mentioned in the

---

[5] Lev 15:16-17; Deut 23:10-11.

[6] Lev 15:18.

[7] Herodotus *Hist.* 2.64.

[8] Num 19:16-19.

[9] John 2:6.

Sibylline Oracles 3,[10] probably reflect ritual purification, including of impurity through seminal emissions. Ritual washing, mentioned in Judith, seems related to purification before eating.[11]

The length of time for purification varied according to the particular kind of uncleanness, as did the ritual requirements. Women in menstruation were deemed to be unclean for seven days and anyone or anything touching them was deemed unclean for that day.[12] People rendered unclean secondarily in this way had to wash their clothes, immerse themselves, and then wait till evening to return to a state of purity.[13] Any man who had sexual intercourse with a woman in menstruation also became unclean for seven days.[14] If a woman's bleeding extended beyond seven days or had some other cause than menstruation, she similarly remained unclean and contagious, and when the flow stopped, she had to wait a further seven days and follow a ritual which included sacrifice to become pure again.[15] Basically the same provisions apply to a man with an irregular discharge such as gonorrhoea and those who touch him.[16] A man who has an emission of semen must bathe and then remains unclean until the evening, along with anything he touches, and so must the woman where the context of the emission was sexual intercourse.[17]

Among the scrolls found at the Dead Sea we have documents which indicate a continuing interest in how these laws were applied and we occasionally see attempts to systematise them or at least to enhance their strictness. Thus we find the seven day purification provision related to corpse impurity being applied to impurity from sexual discharges.[18] Some documents similarly homogenise the requirements applying to gonorrhoea discharges and normal seminal discharges.[19] The *Temple Scroll* extends uncleanness after seminal emission from one to three days, matching the requirements imposed at Sinai according to Exodus, when Moses instructed men to refrain from touching a woman in this sense for three days before the revelatory event.[20] It also declares that all rendered unclean through emissions should be quarantined outside the towns and cities,[21] an

---

[10] *Sib. Or.* 3:591-593.

[11] Jdt 12:7-9.

[12] Lev 15:19-20.

[13] Lev 15:21-23.

[14] Lev 15:24.

[15] Lev 15:25-30.

[16] Lev 15:2-15.

[17] Lev 15:16-18.

[18] 4QRitPur A/4Q414.

[19] *4QTohorot A*/4Q274; 4QD^g/272 1 ii.3-7a.

[20] 11QT^a/11Q19 45.11-12; Exod 19:10-15.

[21] 11QT^a/11Q19 48.14-17.

extension of a ruling in Numbers.[22] These documents, which reflect priestly circles, indicate active concern with getting it right with regard to the boundaries of purity and impurity.

Right order in such things was seen by many as ensuring right order in the rest of society, since such order was demanded by none other than God. Not to follow the rules of purity and purification whether in relation to the temple or in relation to everyday life was therefore an act of disobedience against God. It was sin. Becoming unclean or impure was not a sin in itself, but doing nothing about it or exposing oneself unnecessarily to uncleanness certainly was.

The designation "unclean" can also be used to describe what is forbidden, in particular, certain foods, where distinctions between clean and unclean animals was to be strictly observed.[23] Best known among those prohibitions is the eating of pork. Uncleanness in relation to forbidden food is something different from uncleanness through the processes of life.

Purity and the Temple

As already noted, a person was in a state of uncleanness also when the secretions had some cause other than menstruation or emission of semen. Such was the case with women who bled irregularly and men with discharges from gonorrhoea. Similarly people with skin sores (traditionally called lepers) were also deemed unclean until certified otherwise by the priests, who in this sense exercised a form of medical screening.[24] In the anecdote about Jesus healing a leper we hear Jesus instructing him to go and show himself to the priests for that purpose.[25]

Beside those in a state of temporary impurity, people in a permanent state of what was considered incompleteness, such as the blind, the lame, the castrated, and those born out of wedlock, were not permitted to officiate as priests[26] and on some interpretations were to be banned from the temple altogether, as in the *Temple Scroll*.[27] Such provisions were understood as protecting the temple. The fear was that if the temple were to become less holy or sacred, and be defiled by intrusion of what was impure and incomplete, it might cease to be seen by God as a fit place to dwell.

Some literature from the period, especially from groups, including priests, at odds with the temple establishment, declared that the temple had been contaminated and so abandoned by God (e.g. in the Animal Apocalypse of *1*

---

[22] Num 5:2.

[23] Leviticus 11; Deut 14:3-21.

[24] Leviticus 13 – 14.

[25] Mark 1:40-44.

[26] Lev 21:16-23; cf. also 2 Sam 5:8.

[27] 11QTª/11Q19 45:12.

Enoch[28]). In a similar way sin in the form of neglect of God's commandments, whether moral or ritual, could put not only the temple but also the people and the land out of favour with God. The prohibition of receiving back a divorced wife, for instance, in Deuteronomy, declares that to do so is to "bring guilt on the land"[29] and *Jubilees* deems intermarriage with foreigners as defiling the people, the temple, and the land.[30] The fear of being abandoned, cursed rather than blessed, underlies the seriousness with which many conscientious Jews studied and applied the rules. In this their application to areas sexual played a significant role.

We see this in some of the documents found among the Dead Sea Scrolls which appear to have been written by such a dissenting group. The most careful and conciliatory of these is *4QMMT*, addressed, it appears, to the high priest, in which the author, himself clearly a priest of high standing, explains why he and his group have separated themselves from the temple community. This will have taken place some time around the middle of the second century B. C. E. Among the key issues are concerns relating broadly to sexuality. In particular the author argues against what he sees as a lax attitude towards marriage of both priests and people to non-Jews. The circumstances may reflect marriage to Gentile women taken captive in war, but may also reflect a general trend.

The *Damascus Document*, written some time later, is much more acrimonious, attacking not only the opponents' views, but also the opponents themselves as liars and renegades, a trend which increases in later documents to the extent that the actual issues which began the dispute all but disappear. The practices it cites as traps in which the Jerusalem establishment had entangled themselves include sexual wrongdoing.[31] In particular the author singles out polygyny,[32] which the earlier *Temple Scroll* in its revisions of biblical law had forbidden, but only for the king;[33] sexual intercourse with women during their menstruation;[34] and incest in the form of men marrying nieces, which it argues the prohibition of marrying nephews necessarily implies.[35] Such behaviour, it alleged, defiled the temple.[36]

The issue of engaging in sexual intercourse with a woman during menstruation attacks those who knowingly do so. It is something that might also happen accidentally, in which case there are provisions in biblical law for purification and

---

[28] *1 Enoch* 89:73.

[29] Deut 24:1-4.

[30] *Jub.* 30:1-26.

[31] CD 4.12-19.

[32] CD 4.20-21.

[33] 11QTª/11Q19 57.15-19.

[34] CD 5.6-7.

[35] CD 5.7-11.

[36] CD 4.17-18; 5.6.

no guilt,[37] but this is an example where to render oneself unclean knowingly is reprehensible, thus incurring guilt, because it flouts divine law.[38] Later where it expounds biblical law the *Damascus Document* makes that explicit.[39] When the *Rule of the Congregation* envisions a wife reporting on illicit sexual behaviour by her husband,[40] it may well have intercourse during menstruation in mind. Neglect of menstrual impurity is among the charges levelled against temple priests by the author of the *Psalms of Solomon*;[41] and is possibly also the target of Pseudo-Phocylides.[42]

The disagreement over whether one can marry a niece came up in our discussion of appropriate marriage partners in the previous chapter. The dissenters clearly took the more exclusive approach. It is typical to find both moral issues and purity issues about sexuality lumped together. Neglect of either brought defilement, enough for this group to take the radical step of splitting from their fellow priests. While they would still frequent the temple, it seems that over time this ceased, or at least that they also constructed their own sacred space in the desert at Qumran. They were not the only group of priests and their followers who left the Jerusalem establishment. Early in the second century B. C. E. a group more closely allied with the Ptolemies of Egypt, who had ruled them for over a century up until around 200 B. C. E., than with the Seleucids, who ruled Judea since then, left and set up a temple at Leontopolis in Egypt. Another set up a temple in the Transjordan.

The author of the *Damascus Document* makes much of sexual wrongdoing, constructing a litany of sexual misdemeanours which it sees running through Israel's history, from the Watchers and the women to the kings.[43] Its lists of sins alleged against its opponents include sexual wrongdoing.[44] Its allegation that the congregation of traitors "chose the fair neck"[45] may well already be addressing the theme.

Later in the document the author provides a detailed listing of significant commandments related to the right ordering of religious life, many of them relating to sexual themes in the broad sense. The concern is that these be taken seriously. Not to do so is to bring defilement on oneself and the community. These

---

[37] Lev 15:24.

[38] Lev 18:19; 20:18.

[39] 4QD^a/4Q266 6 ii.1-4; 4QD^g/4Q272 1 ii.7-10; cf. also 4QD^e/4Q270 2 ii.16; *4QHalakhah A*/4Q251 17.2; *4QTohorot A*/4Q274 1 i.5b.

[40] 1QSa/1Q28a 1.11.

[41] *Ps. Sol.* 8:12.

[42] *Ps.-Phoc.* 189.

[43] CD 2.16 – 3.12.

[44] CD 6.14 – 7.4; 8.3-9 / 19.15-21.

[45] CD 1.19.

people saw themselves as taking responsibility for maintaining holiness in the land, not just as something commanded, but as a requirement on the basis of which God would act to restore Israel to blessing and abundance under their leadership.

So the detailed provisions cover seminal emission; menstruation; other male and female discharges; childbirth; forbidden intercourse during menstruation and pregnancy; accusations of adultery; accusations of female unchastity before marriage; rules governing sex with slaves and captive women; guidelines for giving away daughters in marriage and finding appropriate partners; unchastity among daughters at home and abroad and widows; marriage, divorce, and children of divorcees; treatment of prisoners returning home; virgins with no kin and young men with no support; nakedness; and sex on forbidden days and in forbidden places. Similar detailed regulations appear in other documents, showing how seriously both sexual purity and sexual morality were viewed.

Whether sectarian or mainstream, there was widespread concern, especially among priests commissioned with oversight of such provisions, that the boundaries against contamination be drawn as securely as possible, even if that meant constructing a fence, as some put it, around the Law,[46] like a railing constructed two metres from the cliff's edge just to make absolutely sure that no one topples over.

Against Intermarriage with Foreigners

The issue of barriers applied not only to the temple and to avoidable impurity at home, but increasingly became a concern as Jews found themselves engaging with non-Jews both in their homeland and abroad. The issue of intermarriage with foreigners rears its head as early as the accounts of Israel's settlement among the Canaanite peoples according to the early traditions. The fear expressed in them is that intermarriage with the Canaanites would lead to idolatry, as Exodus puts it: prostituting oneself to other gods.[47]

Even before that, already in the account of the transition from Egypt to Canaan, we find the story of Phinehas, who is hailed as a heroic priest for killing a fellow Israelite who had slept with a Midianite;[48] and read of God's alleged instruction to Moses to kill everyone who had engaged in sexual relations with the women of Moab.[49] Phinehas shares with Abraham the honour that his action was reckoned to him by God as righteousness.[50] Indeed, the *Testament of Abraham*, composed in Greek probably in Egypt in the first century C. E., has Abraham behave just like

---

[46] *Aristeas* 139.

[47] Exod 34:11-16; Deut 7:1-6.

[48] Num 25:6-8.

[49] Num 25:1-5.

[50] Ps 106:31; Gen 15:6.

Phinehas, only to have God seek to temper his zeal.[51] According to 1 Maccabees, composed originally in Hebrew some time late in the second or early in the first century B. C. E. and supportive of the Hasmonean dynasty, but surviving only in translation, the leaders of the Maccabean revolt drew inspiration from his zeal.[52] The rewriting of the story in *Pseudo-Philo*, has the prophet Balaam station naked women on the front line to lure Israel's young men into sin,[53] a tradition known also to Philo[54] and Josephus[55] and probably inspired by a later passage in Numbers.[56] Phinehas is again the inspiration for condemning such mixing.[57] Phinehas is also Philo's favourite priest.[58]

Concern with intermarriage to foreigners was central to the reforms of Ezra and Nehemiah, who demanded dissolution of such marriages.[59] Concern that marriage by priests especially, but Jews generally, to foreign women could expose them to illicit knowledge about magic and sorcery, may lie behind the development of the myth of the Watchers in the *Book of the Watchers*.

The concern with intermarriage is taken up in the book of *Jubilees* as a central theme. It takes rules forbidding priests to marry prostitutes and give their daughters to prostitution[60] and applies them to all forbidden women, especially foreign women, and to all Jews on the basis that all Israel is a holy people.[61] The Hebrew word used for a prostitute (*zonah*) and prostitution (*zenut*) was undergoing an expansion, paralleled also in the equivalent terms in Greek (*porne*, *porneia*), so that they now refer to any forbidden woman and any illicit sexual liaison.[62] Intermarriage with foreigners accordingly defiles the people, but also the temple.[63] In its account of Dinah and Shechem,[64] *Jubilees* hails the exploits of Levi and Simeon for killing the people of Shechem after the abduction of Dinah. In its version of the story, the concern is not the abduction, but the intermarriage. It also deletes all reference to circumcision found in the original story, for in its view nothing makes marriage to Gentiles acceptable, not even if they convert and are

---

[51] *T. Abr.* A10:8-9; B12:2-4.

[52] 1 Macc 2:24-25, 54.

[53] *LAB* 18:13-14.

[54] *Virt.* 35-40.

[55] *A.J.* 4.129-144.

[56] Num 31:15-16.

[57] *LAB* 18:13-14; 30:1; 47:1.

[58] *Mos.* 1.301-311; *Mut.* 107-108; *Leg.* 3.242-243.

[59] Ezra 9:1-2; Neh 10:28-30.

[60] Lev 21:7-15.

[61] *Jub.* 16:15-19; Exod 19:6.

[62] *ALD* 6:3-4 / 16-17; *4QMMT* B 75, 82, C 5; cf. also B 8-9; *1 Enoch* 10:9-10; see also the *Book of the Giants*, 4Q203 8.9.

[63] *Jub.* 30:15-16.

[64] *Jub.* 30:1-26; cf. Genesis 34.

circumcised. *Jubilees* sees such marriage as contaminating not only in an ethnic sense and by exposing people to idolatry, but also morally, because it sees Gentiles as engaging in corrupt sexual practices.[65]

Jubilees finds or invents numerous opportunities in its retelling of Genesis to further its message about rejecting marriage to Gentiles. Genealogies are adjusted to hide illicit unions and, where marriage outside the line occurs, *Jubilees* frequently makes it account for the subsequent rise of evil or idolatry, such as in Abraham's family of origin where Nahor had married a Chaldean, as a result of which the idolatry developed from which Abraham has to distance himself.[66] *Jubilees* has Abraham marry Sarah not as his niece and daughter of an idolater, as some read Genesis, identifying her with Iscah,[67] but as his sister. As the author of *Pseudo-Philo* would later assert with regard to Judah and Tamar, Tamar knew that incest was far preferable to marrying a foreigner.[68]

While *Jubilees* found Rebecca's and Isaac's corresponding instruction that Jacob not marry a Canaanite already in Genesis,[69] it includes such warnings already in Abraham's instruction to his descendants.[70] The Canaanites, it alleges, are idolatrous and unclean. We noted earlier that the author rewrites the story of Sarah's abduction by Pharaoh on the one hand to depict it as an act of violence ("by force")[71] and on the other to assure the hearer that absolutely nothing happened between them, so that the matriarch returned undefiled. For her to have been defiled and, further, by a foreigner, would have been a catastrophe. It then freely invents a conversation between Rebecca and Jacob in which she repeats the advice of Isaac and Abraham, adding that Canaanite women are both impure and immoral.[72] By contrast, Esau, whose foreign wives embittered his parents,[73] is the villain who sought to lure Jacob to his ways.[74]

Judah's marriage to Shua, a Canaanite,[75] called Betasuel in *Jubilees*,[76] was the ultimate cause of Judah's shameful demise. Tamar, an Aramean, was deemed an acceptable spouse, who like Joseph's Egyptian wife, Aseneth, fell outside the

---

[65] *Jub.* 20:3-4; 25:1; 27:8.

[66] *Jub.* 11:10.

[67] *Jub.* 12:9; cf. Gen 11:29; Josephus *A.J.* 1.151.

[68] *LAB* 9:5.

[69] Gen 27:46; 28:1; *Jub.* 25:1, 3; 27:10.

[70] *Jub.* 20:4; 22:21.

[71] *Jub.* 13:11, 13; cf. also 1QapGen ar/1Q20 20:14.

[72] *Jub.* 25:1-3.

[73] Gen 26:34-35; 27:46.

[74] *Jub.* 25:8; 27:8; 35:15.

[75] Gen 38:1-4.

[76] *Jub.* 34:20.

forbidden categories. *Jubilees* makes Betasuel to blame for the debacle, including the incest, which becomes its main concern in the instruction which follows.[77]

This hardline stance against intermarriage, which *Jubilees* develops most fully on the basis of the story of Dinah's abduction and Levi's heroic revenge, reappears in the *Aramaic Levi Document* and in the *Testament of Levi* which reworks it within the *Testaments of the Twelve Patriarchs*. The former hails Levi as a hero for killing the Shechemites[78] with no hint of the disapproval reflected in Genesis[79] and so portrays him as forerunner of Phinehas. The concern is marriage of priests' daughters to foreigners, but, as in *Jubilees* and its expansion of the rules about priests, also wider than that, as both the instance of Dinah and also the appeal to Isaac's instruction to Jacob suggest.[80] The text even appears to incriminate Dinah herself,[81] a stance which may be reflected in the fragments of the early second century B. C. E. poet Theodotus (she should have stayed home!)[82] and later in *Genesis Rabbah*.[83] In contrast, in *Pseudo-Philo*[84] she is a model matriarch and in the *Testament of Job* becomes Job's wife.[85]

While *Jubilees* and *Aramaic Levi Document* make Levi the main hero, fitting in his priestly role,[86] elsewhere both Levi and Simeon share the honours as in Genesis[87] or Simeon is alone the hero as in Judith and Theodotus.[88] Mostly Levi and Simeon's revenge for Dinah inspires zealous adherence to Torah, including therefore rejection of foreign marriages. Rarely are the excesses and Jacob's disapproval noted.[89]

In Tobit, on the other hand, the demand, couched as divine command, is not only that Tobias not marry a foreigner, but also that he marry only within his own tribe,[90] an ideal followed also by Judith.[91] This seems more to do with issues of retaining inheritance than just issues of pollution.[92]

---

[77] *Jub.* 41:23-28.
[78] *ALD* 12:6 / 78.
[79] *Jub.* 34:30 and 49:5-7.
[80] *ALD* 6:3-4 / 16-17; 4QLevi[b] ar/4Q213a 3-4 3a.
[81] *ALD* 1:1-3 / 1c 2; Cf. Gen 34:1-3, 5, 13.
[82] Theod. 4 7-9.
[83] Cf. also 4 Macc 18:7-10.
[84] *LAB* 8:6, 8, 11.
[85] *T. Job* 1:5.
[86] *Jub.* 30:18; *T. Levi* 5:3-4; 6:3.
[87] *Asen.* 23:24.
[88] Jdt 9:2-4; *Theod.* 6.
[89] Exception: 4 Macc 2:19-20.
[90] Tob 4:12.
[91] Jdt 8:1.
[92] Tob 4:13.

As noted above, opposition to marriage by both priests and people to Gentiles is a stance strongly advocated in *4QMMT*, which hails Phinehas' exploits.[93] It rewrites the provisions in Deuteronomy about who may join the congregation,[94] deleting the provision for eventual incorporation of Ammonites and Moabites, leaving therefore no room for foreigners and so intermarriage.[95] It takes the prohibitions against mixing different kinds of seeds and animals[96] as equally applicable to people.[97] It appears to treat the practice of taking wives from among women prisoners of war,[98] also as an abomination.[99] To bolster its warning about intermarriage it also cites the faith of Phinehas and Abraham and the failures of David and Solomon.[100]

The interpretation of Deuteronomy 23 played a significant role in defining who may or may not "be admitted to the assembly of the Lord"[101] and to the temple. A total ban on foreigners, as enunciated in *4QMMT*,[102] is reflected also in its comment that letting Gentiles sacrifice is as unacceptable as illicit sex.[103] Like *4QMMT* the document 4QFlor/4Q174, when speaking of the future temple, bans all foreigners.[104] Unlike in Deuteronomy 23 there is no room for Ammonites and Moabites after ten generations,[105] nor for Edomites or Egyptians after three.[106] Foreigners and proselytes are to be excluded. Elsewhere, such as in the *Temple Scroll*, the restrictions are not so harsh. On the one hand, it not only bans all who are in a state of impurity, but also all lepers or infected persons as well as the blind.[107] On the other, women, boys under 20, and proselytes (after three generations) are admissible to the outer court.[108] *4QMMT* similarly bans the blind and deaf from the temple, but on grounds that their disability would prevent them from being able to observe the Law correctly,[109] though they may still have access

---

[93] *4QMMT* C 31-32.

[94] Deut 23:2-4.

[95] *4QMMT* B 39-49.

[96] Lev 19:19 and Deut 22:9-11; cf. 4QD^f/4Q271 3 9-10.

[97] *4QMMT* B 75-82.

[98] Deut 7:6.

[99] *4QMMT* C 4-32 esp. C 6-7.

[100] *4QMMT* C 18-27.

[101] Deut 23:1.

[102] *4QMMT* B 39-49.

[103] *4QMMT* B 8-9.

[104] 4QFlor/4Q174 1-2 i.21 2b-4.

[105] Cf. Deut 23:3-6.

[106] Cf. Deut 23:7-8.

[107] 11QT^a/11Q19 45.7-18.

[108] 11QT^a/11Q19 39.7; 40.6-7.

[109] *4QMMT* B 49b-54.

to sacred food.[110] The *Damascus Document* declares similarly that "the fool or
insane may not enter; and no simple[ton or] ignoramus or one with eyes too weak
to [see or lame or crippled or deaf] or m[ino]r child".[111] We see here another
instance of what originally applied to priests, who could never serve if blind or
deaf, being extended to the whole people.

The strict stance of opposing intermarriage to foreigners reappears in many
other documents among the Scrolls, perhaps directly influenced by *Jubilees*. A
number remain concerned primarily with marriages by priests.[112] Concern about
marrying foreigners was by no means limited to works found among the Dead Sea
Scrolls. When 1 Maccabees reports inappropriate relations with Gentiles, it may
well have intermarriage in mind, especially because it mentions Phinehas' zeal in
the context[113] and alludes to people changing the Law,[114] a common motif among
those criticising laxity in this regard. Concern that teaching authorities are
changing the Law appears also in the *Epistle of Enoch*,[115] though there, as later in
Qumran scrolls, the *Community Rule*[116] and the *Thanksgiving Hymns*,[117] with no
connection to sexual wrongdoing, unlike in *Jubilees*. The issue of marriage to
foreigners may also be reflected in the references to inappropriate mixing in 2
Maccabees.[118]

It resurfaces in *Pseudo-Philo*, not only in its retelling of Phinehas' exploits, but
also, as noted above, in its argument that it was less of an evil for Tamar to have
slept with her father-in-law Judah, than for her to have married a Gentile.[119] It
even takes the extreme position of portraying the vicious rape of the Levite's
concubine in its retelling of Judges 19 as in part deserved because she had had
sexual relations with a Gentile.[120] Its passing over of the accounts of Sarah's and
Rebecca's abductions by Pharaoh and Abimelech may well have been to avoid
soiling his work with potential suggestions of sexual relations with Gentiles.

2 Baruch associates intermarriage with idolatry.[121] Job, in his final instructions
in the *Testament of Job*, warns against intermarriage,[122] as do a number of other

---

[110] *4QMMT* B 54b.

[111] CD 15.15-17; 4QD^a/4Q266 8 i.7-9.

[112] 4QOrd^b?/4Q513; 4QApocrJer C^e/4Q390 2 i. 10; *4QTestament of Qahat*.

[113] 1 Macc 1:11-15; 2:53-54.

[114] 1 Macc 1:45.

[115] *1 Enoch* 98:14-15; 99:1; 104:9-11.

[116] 1QS/1Q28 11.1-2.

[117] 1QH^a vi.15; xii.10.

[118] 2 Macc 14:37-38; 14:3.

[119] *LAB* 9:5.

[120] *LAB* 45:3; 47:8.

[121] *2 Bar* 42:4-5; 48:22-24; 60:1-2; cf. Judg 3:5-6.

[122] *T. Job.* 45:3.

writings, including Theodotus;[123] *Pseudo-Aristeas,* a late second century B. C. E. Jewish work purporting to be written by one of Pharaoh's personnel;[124] *Psalms of Solomon*[125] and *Sibylline Oracles* Book 5.[126] The last two look to a future where no Gentiles will dwell in the land.

The book of Esther celebrates Esther's rise to be Ahasuerus' queen and her influence in rescuing her people from Haman's planned pogrom. It is striking that in the expanded version preserved in Greek this is somewhat turned on its head. Becoming queen is not a reward but the result of her being abducted from her husband, Mordecai, and made to serve in a harem. Accordingly Addition C has her declare her abhorrence of the situation in which she finds herself, where she lives in fear for her life.[127] In her prayer she declares her hatred for "the glory of the lawless" and deplores "the bed of the uncircumcised and of any foreigner".[128] Adding "of any foreigner" means even proselytes are out of the question, as in *Jubilees.*

The *Testaments of the Twelve Patriarchs,* preserved in a Christianised version, also reflects strong opposition to marriage to foreigners. The *Testament of Levi,* which draws on *Aramaic Levi Document,* predicts that future priests would enter such marriages and contaminate themselves with impurities as a result.[129] Its retelling of the slaughter at Shechem exhibits a tension between Jacob's compromise of intermarriage after circumcision of males and Levi's rejection of such marriage.[130] Like *Jubilees,* its source, it makes Judah's marriage to a Canaanite, in defiance of patriarchal law enunciated by Isaac,[131] one of the chief reasons, along with too much wine,[132] for the disasters which followed.[133] Interestingly it portrays Bath-shua as pursuing an equally hard line in opposing intermarriage of Canaanites outside their own.[134] The incorporation of Bilhah and Zilpah into Abraham's family tree, thus no longer to be seen as foreigners, appears directed at dealing with the objection that Jacob slept with foreign woman.[135]

---

[123] Theod. 4 18-21.

[124] *Aristeas* 139, 142.

[125] *Ps. Sol.* 17:28.

[126] *Sib. Or.* 5:264.

[127] Esther C 25 / 14:13.

[128] Esther C 26-28/14:15-17.

[129] *T. Levi* 14:6.

[130] *T. Levi* 5:3-4; 6:3 – 7:4; Gen 34:40.

[131] Gen 28:1.

[132] *T. Jud.* 8:1-2; 11:1-5.

[133] *T. Jud.* 14:6.

[134] *T. Jud.* 10:1-6.

[135] *T. Iss.* 1:10-11.

For Intermarriage with Foreigners

In some instances we appear to have deliberate counterarguments being made in favour of including Gentiles, always on the basis that they join Israel by becoming proselytes. Resistance to the exclusive stance gave birth to some of Israel's best known tales, not least, Esther, Ruth, and Jonah. Joseph's marriage to Aseneth, reported in Genesis,[136] could hardly be denied and, though less prominent, Moses' marriages[137] could also be cited.

For many, not only their intellectual reflection but also their direct experience would have persuaded them that openness was appropriate, not least those who had come to know and respect their neighbours in foreign lands. To such people, those who convert and become proselytes are appropriate marriage partners.

Somewhat unexpectedly, we appear to find some level of tolerance towards marriage to proselytes in what are otherwise exponents of very strict interpretations of the Law. For instance, concern with intermarriage is absent from the legal discussion in the *Temple Scroll* and in both the exhortations and legal expositions in the *Damascus Document*. Both appear to have provisions which allow for incorporating female prisoners of war into families, including even priestly ones.[138] Such prisoners would have inevitably been Gentiles. We must assume in these cases that the authors understand them to have fully embraced Judaism and become proselytes. Thus, unlike *4QMMT* in relation to the assembly and *4QFlor* in relation to the future temple, both of whom revised Deuteronomy 23 to exclude foreigners, the *Damascus Document* clearly includes proselytes. It lists proselytes, as one of four categories of people who belong.[139]

The *Temple Scroll* envisages delineation between the court of the male Israelite over 20 years of age, and that of the women and children, but adds that this was also where proselytes (after the third generation)[140] were permitted. Otherwise foreigners are forbidden entry absolutely. While the *Temple Scroll* cites Exod 34:15-16, which warns about relations with Canaanites, uses sexual language as a metaphor to describe idolatry and forbids intermarriage,[141] the author neither here nor elsewhere makes intermarriage a theme. The only instance is quite telling: it is forbidden for the ruler;[142] not apparently for others. Similarly the *Damascus Document* may well have illicit marriage to foreigners in mind in some instances

---

[136] Gen 41:45.

[137] Exod 2:21; Num 12:1.

[138] 11QT^a/11Q19 63.10-15 ; 4QD^e/4Q270 4 13-19; Deut 21:10-14.

[139] CD 14.4, 6; similarly *4QFour Lots*/4Q279 5 2-6.

[140] 11QT^a/11Q19 39.5; 40:6-7.

[141] 11QT^a/11Q19 2.12-15.

[142] 11QT^a/11Q19 57.15-19.

in its litany of sexual wrongdoing.[143] Thus describing Abraham, Isaac, and Jacob as "friends of God"[144] may have evoked memories of the use of the designation in *Jubilees* which the author knew and cited.[145] Similarly reference to sin in the wilderness and resultant bloodshed[146] may evoke Phinehas' deed. The sins of the kings[147] surely included illicit marriages. Despite this, the author did not make any absolute prohibition which would rule out all marriage to foreigners, provided they converted. No reference is made to such a restriction in its instruction about suitable marriage partners,[148] despite its using the imagery of mixed seed and cloth,[149] which in *4QMMT* serves to justify the ban.[150]

Philo similarly opposed intermarriage with foreigners, indeed, emphasising, like Tobit, that it was preferable to marry within one's extended family,[151] but does not oppose marrying those who convert and accordingly rewrites biblical stories which include Gentile spouses or slaves, like Hagar, Tamar, and Bilhah, to elevate their status, which also raised their respectability in Roman eyes, and show them embracing Israel's faith.[152] Plutarch is probably representative in his advice that a wife adopt her husband's friends and gods,[153] so that our authors would assume that this would be the case with women, for whom, beyond that, no further obstacle such as circumcision would form a deterrent, as it did for men.

This is the stance of Josephus, who is eager to tread sensitively with his Roman audience, but cannot hide his insistence that intermarriage is unconscionable without conversion. We see this in his accounts of the marriages of Drusilla, daughter of Agrippa I. After his death his son, Agrippa 2, acting as a son would on his behalf, gave his sister Drusilla in marriage to "Azizus king of Emesa, who had agreed to be circumcised".[154] She had been betrothed to a certain Epiphanes, son of Antiochus, king of Commagene,[155] but that marriage did not go ahead because he refused to convert. The procurator Felix then fell in love with her, persuaded her to leave Azizus and marry him, an uncircumcised Gentile. Their offspring,

---

[143] CD 2.16b – 3.12a.
[144] CD 3.2-4.
[145] *Jub.* 19:9; 30:20.
[146] CD 3.6-7.
[147] CD 3.9-10.
[148] 4QD^f/4Q271 3 9-10.
[149] Deut 22:10-11.
[150] *4QMMT* B 76-78.
[151] *Spec.* 3.29; 2.126.
[152] *Abr.* 250-251; *Virt.* 223.
[153] Plutarch *Moralia* 140D.
[154] *A.J.* 20.139.
[155] *A.J.* 20.139-140.

Agrippa, together with his wife, were killed when Vesuvius erupted to bury
Herculaneum and Pompeii, which Josephus probably saw as divine judgement.[156]

Throughout his retelling of his people's history Josephus emphasises the
prohibition of intermarriage, citing Jacob's declaration to this effect in the Dinah
story where he was prepared to accept the Shechemites if circumcised;[157]
Samson's fate as the fruit of disregarding it;[158] Solomon's excess and idolatry;[159]
Balaam's strategy of seduction and Phinehas' response;[160] and Ezra's reforms.[161]
In his account Ruth truly converts.[162] Going beyond the biblical history he
mentions with disapproval the intermarriage by priests with Samaritans;[163] the
Tobiad Joseph's obsession with a foreign dancing girl;[164] and the error of Anilaeus
taking a foreign wife.[165] Josephus courts Roman sympathy by depicting this as
respecting ancestral law, a value he knew they espoused, and as having some
parallels in other highly regarded cultures, including a reference to Plato.[166]

The romance, *Joseph and Aseneth*, in the guise and costume of a love story,
takes up what for some was the anomaly that Joseph married Aseneth, a Gentile,
the daughter of the pagan priest of Midian,[167] and makes it a model. For Aseneth
converts, is blessed with heavenly visions, having left her idols behind. Joseph
gladly marries her. In a deft touch, not without irony, Levi, traditionally the
hardliner opposed to such matches, becomes her champion against those who
oppose the match.[168] Marriage to foreigners is affirmed – on the proviso they
convert.

We find the limitation on marriage partners reflected also in papyri, where one
divorce certificate declares the woman free "to marry any Jewish man".[169] Paul's
comment about widows suggests a similar perspective when he writes that those
wanting to remarry should feel free to do so but "only in the Lord".[170] The early
Christian movement will have had to deal with the issue of intermarriage at some
stage, especially as it opened itself to Gentiles, though we find it nowhere

---

[156] *A.J.* 20.144.
[157] *A.J.* 1.338.
[158] *A.J.* 5.286.
[159] *A.J.* 8.192-193.
[160] *A.J.* 4.129-155.
[161] *A.J.* 11.140, 153.
[162] *A.J.* 5.318-340.
[163] *A.J.* 11.302-307.
[164] *A.J.* 12.187.
[165] *A.J.* 18.345.
[166] *Ap.* 2.257-258.
[167] Cf. Gen 41:45.
[168] *Asen.* 22:11-13.
[169] *P. Mur.* 19.
[170] 1 Cor 7:39.

discussed, probably because it may well have been resolved without controversy. In time converts would be deemed to belong to God's people, even without circumcision, the latter an issue of intense controversy in the early years, but not brought into connection with marriage.

In using traditional language of demarcation, contrasting righteousness and lawlessness, light and darkness, Christ and Beliar, faith and unfaith, the temple of God with idols, Paul urges that believers not be yoked with unbelievers.[171] His words come in a passage that appears to have mixed marriages in mind which belong to the concerns about sexual wrongdoing that still concerns him at Corinth.[172] Interestingly, he earlier depicted belonging to God's people as being within a sphere of active holiness which sanctified its members and could even extend that sanctification in some sense to non-believing partners of believers in pre-existing marriages, and to their children.[173]

Holiness Beyond the Temple and Sexual Abstinence

While the temple is the primary holy place, it was not as though Jews believed that God was present only there or that no other holy places existed. Holiness was larger and wider than the Jerusalem temple could encompass. This was true in two different ways: in the extent of the dimensions of the temple itself and in the experience of Jews beyond the temple and Jerusalem and not least in the period after its destruction.

The *Temple Scroll* is so-named because it lays down parameters for an expansion of the temple. One of its most radical assertions is that the holiness of the temple extends to the bounds of the city. The whole city is to be seen as belonging to the temple. The implications are that laws that apply to the temple must now apply to the city as a whole. Nothing unclean or impure must enter it. Should anyone within become impure through unforeseen onset of menstruation or nocturnal emission, they must leave the city until they have returned to purity.[174] It would mean that no sexual intercourse is to take place in the city, nor any other avoidable activity which would cause impurity and so pollution. We find this same view of the city's sanctity presupposed in the *Damascus Document*.[175]

The expansion of the holy also took place at another level, that of time. The book of *Jubilees* declares the Sabbath a holy space where sexual relations must not take place,[176] in other words a time which is to be observed in a state of purity.

---

[171] 2 Cor 6:14 – 7:1.

[172] 2 Cor 12:20-21.

[173] 1 Cor 7:12-14.

[174] 11QT^a/11Q19 45.6-12.

[175] CD 12.1.

[176] *Jub.* 50:8; also 2:25-27.

4QHalakhah A/4Q251 and the *Damascus Document* appear to share this view.[177] The missing words in the prohibition of a man approaching his wife "on the day of xxx" in the fragments of the *Damascus Document* found in cave 4 among the Dead Sea Scrolls[178] probably refer to the Sabbath and the same concern may be reflected where the author writes of defiling sabbaths and festivals.[179] When the document warns men against approaching their wives for illicit sexual intercourse[180] and the author of the Dead Sea Scroll, the *Rule of the Congregation* expresses a similar concern, asking wives to report their husbands,[181] we may well have a similar concern.

Another holy space was the war camp. Understood in Deuteronomy as a place of God's promised presence,[182] it is portrayed in the *War Scroll*, preserved in multiple fragmentary copies among the Dead Sea Scrolls, as a holy place which no people with disabilities, nor men in a state of uncleanness, nor boys, nor women may enter.[183] As in Deuteronomy,[184] newly married men should stay at home with their wives. Banning women almost certainly related to potential pollution through menstruation or through the emissions of sexual intercourse. Similarly the holiness, expressed as reflected in the presence of angels, required that all nakedness be banned from the camp. Accordingly, toilets were to be located 2000 cubits (ca 1 km; 0.6 mile) away from the camp.[185] The *Temple Scroll* demands a distance of 3000 cubits (ca 1500 meters or a mile) from the holy city,[186] a highly problematic distance on the Sabbath day which restricted travel to 1000 cubits!

Nakedness was out of place in holy presence. Perhaps exposing the penis was seen as an act of power where one should be submissive. But nakedness was out of place everywhere except in the intimacy of husband-wife relations. *Jubilees* attacks the spread of the Hellenistic sporting tradition of performing naked.[187] The rule for the sect at Qumran sets punishments for exposing one's penis and also for gesticulating with the left hand, which as in many cultures was to be kept for the dirty tasks and so would be insulting.[188] Inappropriate exposure of nakedness such as in Ham's sin in looking at his father's nakedness with the resultant curse of

---

[177] CD 11.5; 4QD^f/4Q271 5 i.1-2.

[178] 4QD^e/4Q270 2 i.18-19.

[179] CD 12.4; similarly 4QApocrJer C^e/4Q390 2 i.9-10.

[180] 4QD^e/4Q270 7 i.12-13; 4QD^b/4Q267 9 vi.4-5.

[181] IQSa/1Q28a 1.9-11.

[182] Deut 20:1, 4.

[183] 1QM/1Q33 7.3-5.

[184] Deut 24:5.

[185] 1QM/1Q33 7.7.

[186] 11QT^a/11Q19 46.13-16.

[187] *Jub.* 3:30-31.

[188] 1QS/1QS28 7.14, 16-17; similarly 4QD^a/4Q266 10 ii.9-12a; 4QD^e/4Q270 7 i.1-3.

Canaan warranted condemnation,[189] but especially sexual exposure was an abhorrent sin.

Special places of divine presence demanded similar restrictions. The *Rule of the Congregation* lays down rules about who is to be excluded when the congregation gathers for judgement or war, listing a range of people with disabilities, including also the faltering elderly, as well as any man in a state of impurity through discharge or seminal emission.[190] The list of people with disabilities derives from Leviticus,[191] where it applies to priests, but here the community understands its gathering as creating a sacred space. The rationale both here and with regard to the war camp is that God's holy angels are present.[192]

The notion of a temporary abstinence from sexual relations connected with the need to be in a state of purity comes to expression already in the instruction to be given by Moses to the people on approaching Sinai: "The LORD said to Moses: 'Go to the people and consecrate them today and tomorrow. Have them wash their clothes and prepare for the third day, because on the third day the LORD will come down upon Mount Sinai in the sight of all the people".[193] Moses does so: "So Moses went down from the mountain to the people. He consecrated the people, and they washed their clothes. And he said to the people, 'Prepare for the third day; do not go near a woman'."[194] Going near a woman might lead to sexual intercourse, which would then render the men impure. A similar value is reflected in the account in 1 Samuel 21 where in response to David's request that Ahimelech the priest feed his hungry men with the holy bread, the priest first lays down the stipulation "provided that they have kept themselves from women",[195] that is, are in a state of purity, not having had intercourse with women, an assurance David then gives.

Neither instance disparages sexuality or sexual intercourse. It is a matter of being in the right state at the right time and place. As noted above, the three day period of abstinence imposed by Moses at Sinai will have influenced the author of the *Temple Scroll* to require a period of three days instead of just one for men after seminal emission.[196] It also lies behind the requirement of three days' abstinence before the day of the community assembly according to the *Rule of the Congregation.*[197]

---

[189] 4QcommGen A/4Q252.

[190] 1QSa/1Q28a 2.3-4.

[191] 1QSa/1Q28a 1:16-23 also 2 Sam 5:8.

[192] 1QSa/1Q28a 2.8-9; 1QM/1Q33 7.6.

[193] Exod 19:10-11.

[194] Exod 19:14-15.

[195] 1 Sam 21:4.

[196] 11QT^a/11Q19 45.11-12; Exod 19:10-15.

[197] 1QSa/1Q28a 2.4-9.

Such abstinence for the sake of being in a state of purity in preparation to enter holy space finds expression elsewhere. In writing to the Corinthians Paul describes it as appropriate to withdraw from engaging in sexual intercourse in order to engage in a period of prayer.[198] This finds a close parallel in the *Testament of Naphtali* in the *Testaments of the Twelve Patriarchs* where Naphtali both affirms sexual union as an expression of the second great commandment of love of neighbour and cautions that it must always take second place to the first for times of prayer.[199]

Philo speculates about Moses, that he entered such a state of readiness permanently in order to commune with God. In keeping with his psychology of having no dealings with the passions, he depicts Moses as "purifying himself from all the calls of mortal nature, food and drink and intercourse with women",[200] only to acknowledge that this was not sustainable in the long term.[201] It does however reflect the belief that exceptional people like Moses would need to engage in long periods of sexual abstinence. Later rabbinic tradition saw Moses' celibacy similarly.[202] A similar state of celibate holiness may explain why *1 Enoch* depicts the seer as receiving his visions before he was married.[203]

The idea that prophets might need to practice abstinence, at least from time to time, seems to be assumed elsewhere. Already the prophet Jeremiah reports being instructed to remain unmarried.[204] The connection is probably present when Luke depicts the virgin daughters of Philip as prophets in Acts.[205] This suggests an awareness that people called to exceptional tasks might embrace celibacy, either for the duration of the task or the duration of their calling. This was probably related to their need to be constantly in holy places or at least holy or spiritual realms. This makes sense of both prophetic and priestly celibacy, such as that of Nir at his appointment as priest,[206] though, like Philo's Essenes and his Therapeutae,[207] he was already an old man.

When the author of the *Damascus Document* writes of two categories of "men of perfect holiness", those who marry and live in camps and those who do not,[208] he is describing a celibate lifestyle probably related to living in an especially holy

---

[198] 1 Cor 7:5.

[199] *T. Naph.* 8:7-10.

[200] *Mos.* 2.68-69.

[201] *Leg.* 3.145, 147.

[202] *Sifre Num* 12.1.

[203] *1 Enoch* 83:2.

[204] Jer 16:1-4.

[205] Acts 21:9.

[206] *2 Enoch* 71:1-20.

[207] *Contempl.* 68; *Hypoth.* 11.3.

[208] CD 7.4-9; 19.1-5.

place, perhaps at the Qumran site. That would make sense of the reference in Pliny the Elder to a community of celibates there[209] and also of the reports in Philo[210] and Josephus[211] who both mention Essene celibacy, the latter also mentioning the second group who married and presumably lived in small communities across Judea.[212]

While Pliny seems impressed by the absence of women, both Philo and Josephus take this further arguing that the grounds for the Essenes' celibacy lay in the rejection of sexual passion, at least for themselves, and the desire to live in harmonious community, which both believe having women present would ruin because of what they claimed was their contentiousness and lack of self-control.[213] Philo, faced with having to explain how the contemplatives, known by their description as devotees, the Therapeutae and Therapeutrides, included women, does so by depicting them as (safely!) aged virgins.[214] We may suspect that the rationales offered by both authors reflect their own values rather than those of the Essenes. For nothing of this nature appears in the sectarian writings found at Qumran, which are widely attributed to the Essene movement. The *Damascus Document* assumes two kinds of Essenes, the married and the unmarried. Its warnings which follow shortly thereafter[215] imply that it sees a place for men and their families as belonging "in the house of the law".[216] We find no disparagement of sexual passion as present in Philo and Josephus, nor negative views of women in those terms. We shall return to the issue of sexual passion in the next chapter.

One of the striking innovations in the way the book of *Jubilees* retells the stories of Genesis is in its portrait of the garden of Eden. It describes the garden as the holiest place on earth.[217] God had created Adam on the sixth day and then Eve a week later.[218] As we saw in the first chapter, *Jubilees* tells the story in a way that places great value on intimacy and companionship, including sexual intimacy. Only after 40 days does God introduce Adam into the garden, and after 80 days, Eve.[219] This corresponds to the periods of purification required of a woman after birth of a male and female child, respectively.[220] It is a somewhat playful aetiology

---

[209] Pliny *Nat. Hist.* 5.17.

[210] *Prob.* 75-91; *Hypoth.* 11.

[211] *B.J.* 2.119-161; *A.J.* 18.18-22.

[212] *B.J.* 2.160.

[213] Philo *Hypoth.* 11.14; Josephus *B.J.* 2.121.

[214] *Contempl.* 2, 11-40, 63-90.

[215] CD 19.33b – 20.1a, 8b-13.

[216] CD 20.13.

[217] *Jub.* 3:12; 4:26; 8:19; similarly 4Q265/4QSD 7 ii 11-14.

[218] *Jub.* 2:14; 3:1.

[219] *Jub.* 3:8-9.

[220] Lev 12:2-5; *Jub.* 3:10-12.

for that provision, and fitting for the way *Jubilees* treats the garden, namely as a sanctuary. During their time in the garden-temple they are chaste. They remain in a state of purity. Only after they leave the garden do they resume sexual intercourse and only then did Eve give birth to Cain and Abel.[221] In *Jubilees* we are dealing with another instance of the right place and time. In holy place and, for the author, holy time, sex was out of place. In ordinary time and place sex belongs and is affirmed as a normal part of life. Indeed one of the special features of this work is its affirmation of marital intimacy, and not just limited to a focus on procreation.

Others, too, envisaged creation of man and woman outside the garden, but none, with one exception,[222] depicts the garden as a temple. We are left to speculate how *Jubilees* might envisage the future, especially if it might have seen future hope entailing a return to paradise. In one of its predictions it writes of people being like children.[223] This might indicate a return to innocence, but if so this would be rather unusual. The closest we come to such a notion in Jewish literature of the period is in the *Book of Jewish Antiquities*, also noted for affirming sexual relations in this life, which saw the future abode of the righteous as a "place of sanctification",[224] and in Book 2 of the *Sibylline Oracles* which has no sex in the garden, without declaring it a temple, but describes the future age as one where there will be "no marriage, no death, no sales, no purchases".[225] The *Testaments of the Twelve Patriarchs* appears to stand under the influence of *Jubilees* and promises re-entry into paradise.[226] Despite its strong affirmation of marital love, amid all its warnings about women, we find no reference to marriage, sexual relations, fertility or abundance in its images of the age to come. In Josephus who appears to draw on *Jubilees'* account of creation, the garden is not a sacred place, a temple.

Celibacy was not a normal option for people brought up on the creation stories and the imperative expressed in Genesis, "Be fruitful and multiply".[227] That was a mandate for all, so that any departure from the norm would have to be warranted by exceptional circumstances or a special call. According to *Pseudo-Philo* people should multiply like spawning fish.[228] In it Amram vehemently confronts the strategy some were considering of not marrying so that the Egyptians could not

---

[221] *Jub.* 3:34-35; 4:1.

[222] 4Q265/4QSD 7 ii 11-14.

[223] *Jub.* 23:28.

[224] *LAB* 19:12-13; 26:13; 33:5.

[225] *Sib. Or.* 2:328.

[226] Cf. *T. Levi* 18:10-11; *T. Dan* 5:12-13.

[227] Gen 1:28.

[228] *LAB* 13:10.

take their offspring.[229] As we have seen, its hero, Tamar, did better to sleep with Judah than to consider celibacy or marrying a foreigner.[230] The mandate to propagate features regularly through the literature of the time.[231] It was also the official Roman agenda set by Augustus, who required all men and women of fertile age to marry and bear children.[232] Plato had also insisted on it.[233] Philo justifies his beloved Essenes and Therapeutae and Therapeutrides by noting that they were past their fertile years and many of them had done that duty.[234] Procreation was paramount, not only as the sole basis for engaging in sexual intercourse, but also because God commanded it. To do otherwise was very odd.

One of the difficulties in discussing long term sexual abstinence in these ancient texts is our inevitable tendency to think of priestly vows of permanent celibacy when celibacy is discussed. Most celibacy in the texts we are considering is not of that nature. Before we turn to Christian texts which appear to reflect interest or espousal of longer term celibacy, we turn to how most Jews saw the future and the role of sex, marriage, and family life within it.

Sex and the Future

Most expressions of future hope in Jewish literature of the period paint the future as fulfilling the dreams for the present. Sometimes this is almost literally the restoration of peace in the land, centred around the holy city and the temple. That may be associated with some divine intervention through angels, and through human agents such as a Messiah, usually like David, who would overcome enemies. Prophetic hopes of restoration entailed a return of all who had been deported or banished and celebration of peace and joy. Sometimes it had a place for Gentiles who would finally behave as they should, as Israel's friends and admirers, learning God's ways of peace.

Visions of the future usually went beyond literal description into fantasy and symbol, or at least, the fantastic, including the promise of huge harvests of fruit and wine. Abundance regularly included abundant offspring among animals and, not least, humans. Some form of resurrection is often assumed and associated with it, ideas of transformed existence. This could mean life as it is now, but mostly it meant being in a transformed state, sometimes angel-like. Some texts speak of living forever; others of living for a thousand years. The same texts usually combine this with visions of abundant offspring, so that length of life does not

---

[229] *LAB* 9:2.

[230] *LAB* 9:5.

[231] E.g. *1 Enoch* 67:13; 65:12; *2 Enoch* 42:11; 71:37; *Sib. Or.* 1:65; *Ps.-Phoc.* 176.

[232] *Lex Iulia de maritandis ordinibus* 18 B. C. E., updated in *Lex Papia Poppaea* 9 C. E.

[233] *Leg.* 838-839.

[234] *Contempl.* 13, 18, 68; *Hypoth.* 7:3.

seem to have triggered the thought that producing progeny might be superfluous. Nothing suggests an absence of sexual intimacy.

Thus many visions of the future reproduce distinctions between ordinary space and holy space. For there will be a renewed temple and accordingly a sensitivity to what is in place and out of place in the sacred. Sexual engagement would be appropriate in ordinary everyday life but purity and purification would be required for entry into the temple.

People hoped for a future where what should be now finally will be, even if at times their depictions take on dimensions of the marvellous and fantastic. Thus already the earliest section of *1 Enoch*, the Book of the Watchers, looks to a future of abundance: the righteous "will live until they beget thousands, and all the days of their youth and their old age will be completed in peace".[235] Its eschatological image of paradise envisages a separate sanctuary, which the righteous may enter, but which is a special place beside that of their daily life.[236]

. Future hope in the documents found at Qumran similarly envisages a new or renewed or new temple with all the appropriate restrictions for entry, beside the land and its people at peace and enjoying abundance and fertility. The *Treatise of the Two Spirits* which the author has incorporated into later copies of the *Community Rule* speaks of "healing and a spirit of peace in length of days and fruitful offspring with all everlasting blessings, eternal enjoyment with endless life, and a crown of glory with majestic raiment in eternal light".[237] The *Damascus Document* speaks of the righteous remnant filling the face of the world with their offspring.[238] The *Pesher on Psalms* (4QpPs^a/4Q171), an application of Psalm 37 to the author's setting, promises returnees that they will live for a thousand generations, as does the *Damascus Document* similarly,[239] and that they and their seed will repossess the inheritance of Adam forever and take control again of the holy mountain.[240] Living for a thousand generations and in a transformed, radiant state, in no way appears to compromise family life and fertility. Indeed, one of the documents draws on the promise in Exodus of a future without miscarriage and infertility,[241] to declare that the presence of God and the holy angels will guarantee that there will be no miscarriages.[242] Abundant offspring was a common theme.[243]

---

[235] *1 Enoch* 10:17-18.

[236] *1 Enoch* 24 – 25.

[237] 1QS/IQ28 4.6b-8; partly preserved in 4Q257 5.4-5.

[238] CD 2.11b-12a.

[239] CD 7.6 / 19.1-2.

[240] 4QpPs^a/4Q171 1-10 iii. 1-2a, 10-11.

[241] Exod 23:26.

[242] *11QSefer ha-Milhamah*/11Q14 1 ii.11, 14b // *4QSefer ha-Milhamah*/4Q285 8 8, 10-11.

[243] Cf. also 4QInstr^g/4Q423 3 1-5 / 1QInstr/1Q26 2 2-4; 11QT^a/11Q19 59.12.

2 Baruch, which promises fantastic harvests and abundant wine, similarly promises that in those days childbirth will be without pain,[244] despite its understanding that people will not grow old[245] and will be like angels.[246] Wisdom promises that infertile women will be able to conceive.[247] Life at peace in the land, including normal family life and sexual relations, is the common assumption,[248] and may include imagery of a garden of paradise, Eden restored.[249] Philo, too, embraces an eschatology of fertility and fulfilment,[250] also drawing on the promise in Exodus to declare that "No man shall be childless and no woman barren".[251]

The notion of a transformed bodily existence, which often accompanies these fantastic hopes, derives in part from Daniel[252] and in turn from Zoroastrian notions of a glorified bodily state. The most common understanding of resurrection, in that sense, is not of a resuscitated physical body, but of a new or renewed body. Thus the *Community Rule*, cited above, speaks of being clothed in a raiment of light.[253] The work, the *Wiles of the Wicked Woman*, found at Qumran speaks of "those who shine brightly".[254] The *Epistle of 1 Enoch* promises that the righteous will shine like the stars of heaven.[255] This belief is equally evident in early Christian texts where Paul speaks of a spiritual body, not a physical one of flesh and blood;[256] the transfiguration story in Mark foreshadows the appearance of Jesus' resurrection body at the parousia as shining;[257] and Matthew's interpretation of the parable of the weeds depicts the righteous as going to shine like the sun.[258] Being like angels according to *2 Baruch* did not mean abandoning family and sexual relations, as its promise of painless childbirth indicates.[259] Most depictions of the glorious righteous go hand in hand, as we have seen, with promises of abundant offspring.

There is an exception to this inclusive vision of the future. Its clearest expression, and perhaps its only expression, comes to us in early Christian

---

[244] *2 Bar* 73:7.

[245] *2 Bar* 51:16.

[246] *2 Bar* 51:9-10.

[247] Wis 3:13.

[248] E.g. Bar 2:34; Tob 13:5, 11, 13-17; *Sib. Or.* 3:767-795; 4:45; 5:420-421; *Parables of Enoch / 1 Enoch* 39:10; 43:4; 45:5-6; 51:1-54; Ezra 9:8; *2 Bar.* 51:9-10, 16.

[249] *1 Enoch* 60:8, 23; 61:12; similarly 4 Ezra 7:119-126.

[250] Philo *Praem.* 98-105, 108-109.

[251] Philo *Praem.* 107 Exod 23:26.

[252] Dan 12:3.

[253] 1QS/1Q28 4.5.

[254] *4QWiles of the Wicked Woman*/4Q184 1 7b.

[255] *1 Enoch* 104:2-6.

[256] 1 Cor 15:35-49.

[257] Mark 9:2-3; Matt 17:2.

[258] Matt 13:43.

[259] *2 Bar.* 73:7.

tradition, represented in a saying attributed to Jesus, but also underlying Christian writing elsewhere. In response to being teased by Sadducees about his belief in resurrection, who asked what would happen to a woman widowed seven times in the life to come, Jesus is reported as declaring: "When they rise from the dead they neither marry nor are given in marriage, but are like angels in heaven".[260] The issue is not weddings but sexual intercourse. There will be none, for all shall be as angels, who when properly behaving, unlike the Watchers, do not engage in sexual activity. Luke interprets the saying along the lines that people will live forever and so not need to produce progeny and so not need to have sex,[261] the limited view of the role of sexual intercourse which underlies what Enoch was similarly told to put to the Watchers,[262] and which matched popular philosophical values in Luke's day. That view assumes: no need of procreation; therefore no need for sex; indeed no need for women! It does not appear to have been Mark's meaning. Rather the age to come would be one where sexual intercourse would cease to be because people would take on a new form of being like that of angels.

It is possible that this was also a notion of the life to come which no longer retained the structure of the present, of sacred and non-sacred space, but saw all as sacred space, as holy. The Book of Revelation assumes a future garden paradise without a temple.[263] One can only speculate that if one combined *Jubilees'* understanding of the garden paradise as a temple with hope for return to paradise, then the result would indeed be a holy place where sexual relations had no place. One might also see a connection leading in this direction where people envisaged the life to come as an eternal Sabbath, as in Hebrews, if this were combined with the conviction that one should desist from sexual relations on the Sabbath. Even if this is so, it seems that early in the Christian tradition some, perhaps already Jesus, envisaged the future in such terms, at least as a transformed existence where sexual relations ceased to be relevant.

Celibacy Now and Then

Belief in a future without sex may explain why some believers saw it as their lot to live already now as they would then, and others, that they should seek to persuade all to so live. Paul resists those who were seeking to do the latter. He argues that in the interim world which God created sexual relations in proper order had their place,[264] but it is clear that he shares the view that marriage can only be for the short term of this present age and would have no relevance in the age to come. It is

---

[260] Mark 12:25.
[261] Luke 20:34-36.
[262] *1 Enoch* 15:4-7.
[263] Rev 21:22–22:5.
[264] 1 Cor 7:1-6.

better, then, if one can, not to become embroiled in marriage and to leave women alone, not to touch, that is engage sexually, with them.[265]

It is very likely that Paul's own expressed preference for celibacy reflected both his belief that time was nearing its end and a new era was about to begin and that that era would not entail marriage or sexual relations. Both aspects appear to have played a role. Had the issue been only the shortness of time, but included belief in ongoing marital relations, then they could continue to claim a place of significance. Paul does not see it that way. While resisting those who denigrated marriage and sexual relations and countering their stance with his conviction about divine order for the present age, he sees little point in people entering marriage given the circumstances and the nature of the life to come. His affirmation of the present order as God's creation allows him to reassure those who were desperate to marry, that to do so was not sin.[266] There was a choice. For him, it was to live now as he would then. Beyond identifying his view of the age to come as without marriage and sexual relations, there are few clues concerning how he understood it and why he understood it that way.

He certainly did not entertain resurrection life as a simple reconstitution of the human body. Rather, his Christian tradition reflected those Jewish understandings of the age to come as one of a different order of being. One of the foundational texts of resurrection belief, Dan 12:3, already points far beyond notions of physical resurrection. It is also likely that his presuppositions about the holy, which we must assume were deeply ingrained, influenced his understanding. Here his notion of sexual abstinence for a period of prayer[267] is very suggestive. It is not far beyond that to claim that being permanently in holy presence would imply permanent abstinence. That would not be understood as being in reconstituted flesh and having to engage in suppression of sexual passion, but rather of being in a form of existence where the issue would not arise.

Hints of the sense of permanently being in holy presence appear elsewhere. As already noted, the Book of Revelation clearly envisages future hope as being in paradise, perhaps like that of *Jubilees*, in which there is no separate temple, but only divine presence. Normal presuppositions about appropriate behaviour in holy space would lead to the conclusion that sexual relations would, of course, be out of place. When it refers to 144,000 who had not "defiled themselves with women",[268] which should not be taken as misogynist disparagement but as cultic language, referring to the usual impurity issues associated with sexual intercourse, it may well have in mind those believers who saw themselves called to live in the present

---

[265] 1 Cor 7:1, 7-8, 26-35.

[266] 1 Cor 7:9, 28, 36.

[267] 1 Cor 7:5.

[268] Rev 14:4.

as they would in the age to come. They are joined by thousands of others, not lesser Christians, but people not so called.[269]

Anyone, in addition, embracing *Jubilees'* notion of the Sabbath as similarly holy and requiring similar abstinence and seeing the age to come as an eternal Sabbath would reach a similar conclusion. However we lack evidence that Paul and his fellow believers saw the Sabbath in those terms.

It is tempting to treat Jesus' celibacy and John the Baptist's similarly to Paul's, but that is inadvisable. Paul's belonged to a stance which he commended to others, while opposing those who would command it of others. For neither of Jesus nor of John do we find evidence of such commending. At most one could speak of Jesus challenging some to abandon the trappings of family, including, it appears, sometimes their spouses and children. That challenge may also derive from a sense of the urgency of living in the last days, but his call could also entail people following him and then going on mission along with their wives. His choice to be celibate appears to be closely related to his special role and then not, as Philo's Moses, in order to receive divine revelation, but in order to carry out his mission unhindered. At age 30 when most began a family he chose a role which separated him from everyday life and enabled him to pursue an itinerant preaching and healing ministry.

The enigmatic saying which Matthew appends to the controversy about divorce, has Jesus state: "There are eunuchs who have been so from birth, and there are eunuchs who have been made eunuchs by others, and there are eunuchs who have made themselves eunuchs for the sake of the kingdom of heaven".[270] In its third category it appears to be employing the eunuch metaphorically to refer to people who have chosen to live a life of sexual abstinence for the sake of the kingdom of God, such as Jesus, himself, who may even have coined the saying in part to defend his choice. Literal castration is most unlikely. The saying is striking in using the figure of the eunuch. Eunuchs could be scandalous figures, though neither of the first two categories seems to be depicted in that light.

Perhaps even more interesting is the setting in which we find the saying. Before it we read: "Not everyone can accept this teaching, but only those to whom it is given," and after it: "Let anyone accept this who can".[271] Both seem designed to ward off any suggestion that all should become such eunuchs. Paul had a similar concern when noting his own option for singleness when he wrote: "I wish that all were as I myself am. But each has a particular gift from God, one having one kind and another a different kind".[272] Almost certainly some were wanting to go much further than that and demand celibacy of all, which both texts resist.

---

[269] Rev 7:4-11; 14:1-5.

[270] Matt 19:12.

[271] Matt 19:11, 12b.

[272] 1 Cor 7:7.

John's celibacy is likely to have been similar to that of Jesus. They were, after all, closely connected and for some time together. For neither does the issue of sacred space or sacred time, however, appear to have played a role. For both, the immediacy and urgency of impending divine intervention coloured their decision and drove their action. For John our data is in any case minimal. In the case of Jesus we must deduce from what followed his death that he was among those who believed in resurrection and, given the way the early traditions envisaged resurrection, it was likely to have been closer to beliefs in a new order of creation than of a reconstituted physicality. If the statement attributed to him about the absence of sexual relations in the age to come[273] has some correspondence with what he believed or may have said, then his vision of the future belonged with Paul's and did not envisage such relations. On this we can only speculate, although one may assume some degree of continuity between Paul's views and those of Jesus, given the time span and the connections. While Jesus, too, may have seen himself living in the present as he would in the future, as apparently did Paul, nothing of what survives provides evidence of this.

Some later texts which affirm celibacy or at least envisage it for the future appear to draw on speculation that the end will be a return to the beginning, so that separate male and female will return to one as in Gen 1:26. There were streams of speculation also in the Greco-Roman world about return to a single androgynous (male and female) being, though for most it was seen as a return to the highest form of human existence: male. Jewish and Christian variants of this idea depended on Genesis and so envisaged that return as reincorporation of the female back into the male Adam. Thus people acclaimed the good news that women would be elevated to male status. The Gospel of Thomas speaks of Mary being made male.[274] A similar notion may lie behind the depiction of Aseneth in God's presence as male.[275] This was at least code for her full acceptance on the same basis as men. Abandoning head scarves in worship at Corinth may derive from similar beliefs. Reaching such a level of reintegration of female within the male could have led some to believe that therefore sexual relations should be abandoned as belonging to the divided state which they had transcended. This was certainly not the view of Aseneth or, at least, the romance's author, who shortly after celebrates sexual union in marriage.

As Jews encountered learned discourse in the Greco-Roman world, they increasingly took up the latter's concern with proper management of the passions or emotions. Beside anger, grief, joy, craving for food, or indulgence in excessive drinking, was naturally the issue of what to do with sexual feelings. In the chapter

---

[273] Mark 12:25.

[274] *Gos. Thom.* 114.

[275] *Asen.* 15:1.

which follows we turn to Jewish and early Christian appropriation of these concerns.

Passions and Persons

Living in the Hellenistic World

A large number of Jews, indeed, probably most, lived outside their traditional homelands, far from Jerusalem and its temple, in both east and west. In the east these included families who had never returned from the deportations in the sixth century B. C. E. For others, especially in the west, a mixture of trading interests, mercenary resettlements, deportations, and adventure led to the growth of large populations of Jews in major metropolises like Alexandria in Egypt, Antioch in Syria, Tarsus in Asia Minor (present day Turkey), and Rome.

More than most other diaspora peoples far from home, they mostly had regular contact at least with Jerusalem because of the pattern of annual pilgrimages to festivals. Conversely we find reference to many different cultural communities of Jews in Jerusalem, itself, reflecting their diverse origins,[1] many of them with Greek as their first language, rather than the Aramaic of their homeland. Within the bounds of the empire Rome largely succeeded in keeping travel safe from pirates and marauders, which thus supported travel and trade. This in turn offered many opportunities for individuals wanting, for instance, passage by sea.

Living in foreign environments had for many transformed into a sense of feeling quite at home, especially since in many contexts settlement went back generations. Generally accommodation could be found for their special traits, such as not working on the Sabbath, and being selective about foods and marriage partners. From time to time difference was seen by locals as a threat, and signs of antisemitism reach back at least two centuries before the turn of the era. Jewish communities were mostly close knit. People imagine things when they lack

---

[1] Cf. Acts 2:9-11; 6:9.

information and have limited interchange. Success in trade and finance already then aroused suspicions of undue influence. The imaginings about the Jews were at times quite bizarre, such as the allegation that they worshipped a goat.

Governance, first under the Ptolemies till ca. 200 B.C.E. and then under the Syrian Seleucids, both being Greek regimes as a result of Alexander the Great's generals dividing up the spoils of empire, will have brought high levels of contact among the powerful, who were also usually the best educated. Learning statecraft went along with learning wisdom about successful living. The fruits of such interchange are apparent in much earlier times, not least in the Book of Proverbs, where much of it is international and paralleled in ancient Egyptian texts. Such learning would have blossomed in the centuries after Alexander, especially since the Hellenistic rulers made a point of parading Greek fashion and culture.

It caused a crisis in the homeland as it intensified early in the second century. There were those who adopted Hellenistic fashion in dress and lifestyle and at the same time others who saw such influence as a threat. Competing interests among regional ruling families and among leading priests, and financial pressures, both on the Seleucid regime and from it, provoked the revolt led by Judas Maccabeus in 167 B. C. E. In three and a half years it succeeded in restoring and rededicating the temple which had been desecrated by imposition of idolatrous imagery and pig sacrifices, a liberation still celebrated in the Jewish festival of Hanukkah. Only to a limited degree was the conflict really about Hellenistic cultural influence. In the decades and centuries which followed that influence is evident across most parties to some degree, a little like the globalisation of American culture in the contemporary world.

Finding Common Ground

What occurred in Judea in the second century B. C. E. happened in different ways in the Jewish settlements scattered across the empire. Learning the local language meant in most instances learning Greek. Local Jewish leaders would rub shoulders in commerce and governance with their peers in the broader community. Commitment to learning within Jewish communities inevitably meant some interchange with learning in those broader communities. Informally and sometimes formally the powerful Greek ideas about statecraft and about how to live would filter through into Jewish schools and Jewish thought.

At the interface of cultures many Jews would be appalled at blatant disregard for what they deemed divine order. Images of gods and goddesses or of emperors, nakedness, especially in sports, bawdy theatre, sexual promiscuity, including prostitution, male and female, and wild parties characterised by excessive drinking and debauchery – these were enough for many to want to have nothing to do with foreigners. Such separateness, seen as a claim to superiority, seeded hatred among many who observed it.

Yet there were many Jews who welcomed the new. Sometimes the influence was incidental, almost by osmosis. One can image that sharing the same language would have led to sharing ideas and images without even being aware of what was going on. But at a more serious level, there was common ground, because within Hellenistic culture were some who also deplored its excesses and at least questioned its proliferation of deities. In learned circles people would encounter the great thinkers who had written in Greek and whose ideas, even if second-hand and somewhat garbled, had entered public discourse. In the intellectually sophisticated context of Alexandria, home to Jews in the hundreds of thousands, some may well have even had access to its famous library and been able to read for themselves the works of the great philosophers like Plato and Aristotle, and the treatises of Stoics, Epicureans, and Neo-Pythagoreans. Much that they read or at least heard about would have seemed not only compatible with their own convictions, but also useful in both elaborating and propagating them. That included on areas such as sexuality, because the popular philosophers of the period concentrated primarily on wisdom about how to live, and on emotional health in particular.

For some the similarities were so impressive that they seriously claimed that Plato must have read Moses. Usually, however, the engagement entailed saying yes and no. Thus Philo takes up the Platonic notion of invisible "ideas" functioning as patterns after which the physical manifestations, the "real", are formed, like shadows thrown by a fire onto the roof of a cave, and employs it in his exposition of the Genesis creation stories. It enables him to harmonise to some extent the two Genesis accounts. The heavenly human being as a genus incorporates male and female, as in Gen 1:27. Genesis 2 then reports how this became "real" through the formation of the man and the woman.

Yet Philo pours scorn on the creation myth propounded by Aristophanes in Plato's *Symposium*, which justifies homosexual love between men and women beside heterosexual love on the basis of a myth which portrays them as lost halves trying to find each other.[2] Nor could Philo quite go along with Plato's theory that woman came into existence as a devolution from man among men who were failures, starting a slide downwards which eventually produced animals and the lowly snakes.[3] Philo's faith knew that God created woman. His exposition of "Let us" as indicating helpers who are responsible for potential faultiness in humans[4] is still a long way from Plato's view that God left such creation for others to do.[5] Yet

---

[2] *Contempl.* 50-63; cf. Plato *Symp.* 189-193.

[3] Plato *Tim.* 42B, 91A.

[4] *Opif.* 72-75; *Conf.* 179; *Fug.* 71-72; similarly *Mut.* 30-31.

[5] *Tim.* 41D.

Philo, like Josephus, shared the views about women of many of his learned contemporaries, fed on such philosophy, including that of Aristotle, who deemed the female "a defective male".[6] Accordingly woman is inferior, lacks control of passion and intellect, and so woman serves Philo as a symbol of the body, whereas man serves as a symbol of the mind.

Plato's own views in his *Laws*, condemning same-sex relations,[7] found warm acceptance among Jewish writers, who also embraced his arguments, which included that sex should be only for propagation of the species and that animals do not engage in such pairing,[8] a claim we know to be false. Ejaculation in any context other than in marriage for the purpose of bringing children into the world was contrary to nature and so, wrong.[9] That was a strong "no" to not only same-sex relations, but also masturbation, sex with slaves and prostitutes, and indeed all forms of sexual gratification for its own sake, including intercourse during menstruation and pregnancy, and was, by implication, a rejection of contraception. Plato's emphases seemed to cohere well with the command in Genesis that people should be fruitful and multiply,[10] especially when read as defining sex's role.

Plato, however, could contemplate sexual intercourse as legitimate even after the period of people's fertility, during which that was possible and its main aim, as long as it was not excessive.[11] Yet much of the philosophical discourse of the time espoused a utilitarian view of sex: sex was designed for the work of propagation, not for play. As we have seen, for Philo that does not mean denying its pleasure, but the pleasure is nature's way of achieving the end of propagation, and not something to be made a goal in itself. Philo's comments in this regard are part of his exposition of Gen 2:24, which stands at the climax of Genesis 2, that deals not with propagation but with companionship. The focus on companionship tends to be lost in most discussions. Accordingly, Philo deemed intercourse with sterile women, including post-menopausal women, like intercourse with menstruating women, though not, it appears pregnant women, as wasting seed and indulging in sex just for pleasure.[12] Yet some valuing of companionship remains: he does not go so far as insisting that men divorce sterile wives, nor does he argue that such couples should abstain from sexual intercourse.[13]

There were extreme views, such as those attributed to Pythagorean philosophy. They believed that intercourse should not only focus solely on propagation, but

---

[6] *Gen. an.* 737A.28.

[7] *Leg.* 636, 838.

[8] *Leg.* 836C.

[9] *Leg.* 838E-839A.

[10] Gen 1:28.

[11] *Leg.* 784E3-785A3; 783E4-7; 784B1-3.

[12] Philo *Spec.* 3.34, 36; *QG* 1.27.

[13] Philo *Spec.* 3.35.

also be a low-key affair, enabling a smooth passage of the soul into matter. It should not be something turbulent or boisterous, which might harm the soul and create disharmonies bound to harm society later in life. Ocellus and Charondas, the Neo-Pythagoreans active in our period, opposed any intercourse not for propagation, and influenced the Stoic philosophers, Seneca and Musonius Rufus to the same view. Most Stoics did not go that far, and, unlike their founder, Zeno, strongly affirmed marriage as belonging to divine order and emphasised the importance of partnership. Paul mirrors Stoic values when he writes to the Corinthians about mutual giving between husband and wife, including in sexual intimacy.[14] Cynics, like the second century C. E. Epictetus, were more pessimistic about marriage, seeing it as a distraction for a philosopher, a view also matching Paul's arguments in the same chapter that marriage divided a man's attention, which might otherwise be solely on God.[15]

The Stoic emphasis on order in family and community, indeed, in the universe, merged well with the faith in divine law at the heart of Judaism. Those Stoics who used theological language to speak of the divine penetrating all things and holding all things together seemed very close to Jewish belief in creation. Proper ordering of society, whether expressed in Stoic terms or in those of Aristotle, was a value Jews could easily embrace. Teachings about roles of husbands and wives, children, and slaves, were easily transferrable, as Christians also found, when in Colossians and Ephesians, but also in 1 Peter, they accommodated them to their new form or offshoot of Judaism, as we saw in the chapter on households above. The respected and respectable in the best of the Roman world easily became the benchmark for Christian households and enabled them to assert that they were not an oddity but models of virtue.

Managing Sexual Passion

The theme of order and management was inseparable from the theme of self-management and, in that, the secret was to maintain order and respectability. The rash and unpredictable had no place. As in a household and in the state, all parts within a person needed to be kept in their place to sustain the harmony of the whole. Far from a fetish about control, such concern was at the very least about survival in a world of vicissitudes and unpredictability. Life was fragile, exposed to a wide range of dangers from which most in the modern developed world are well protected, but, beyond that and partly because of it, people were regularly having to cope with loss and grief, death and disaster. Emotions should be ruled, not rule. The best way to make one's journey through the challenge of life was to

---

[14] 1 Cor 7:3-4.
[15] 1 Cor 7:32-35.

protect oneself against the vulnerability of being overcome with emotion, pain or pleasure. Moderating one's responses in order to avoid being carried away was an essential life-skill. This applied across the range of emotional responses, but especially to sexual passion.

For all the fun and fascination with dramas based on men or women falling victim to the fate of overwhelming feelings, philosophers, including Plato, Aristotle, the Stoics, the Epicureans and their schools, all set about bursting the illusion of people being victims of fate and calling them in various ways to take responsibility for themselves. The psychologising of mythology which we find, for instance in Euripides, about the tormented soul knowing what is right and not able to do it or not knowing what is wrong and yet doing it, made much sense.[16] Paul employs it to make his case about the impotence of human will to keep the Law.[17] The philosophers' focus, however, was on what to do with such assaults on the self and not on accommodation to them. Some, like the Epicureans, even disputed alleged interventions by gods and belief in an afterlife and argued instead that people should make their own destiny in this life by pursuing true pleasure. To others this sounded like an invitation to extravagance: "Eat, drink, and be merry, for tomorrow we die"; but this was a misrepresentation. If anything, Epicureans were more cautious about sexual passions than Stoics and rejected excess as a dead end that would not achieve true pleasure. Their advice bore an uncanny similarity to the advice of the author of Ecclesiastes to make the most of one's mortal life and its opportunities. Seeking a sense of wellbeing was then as now an attractive philosophy for life.

Some Jewish authors, particularly those influenced by the more acceptable philosophies, such as that of the Stoics, or in touch with schools of international wisdom, took up the emphasis on passions as dangerous. When Ben Sira wrote of sexual passion as potentially a consuming fire,[18] he was drawing on an image already employed in the Jewish wisdom of the Book of Proverbs written long before.[19] He follows its psychology of the attractiveness of the forbidden: the adulterer finds forbidden bread sweet.[20] Excess was harmful, not only in that it might lead to sexual engagement with prostitutes and other's men's wives;[21] it was also seen as harmful within one's own marriage. For it led to lack of control and so to behaviour which brought shame on oneself and one's own and might lead to surrendering control to women, as in the case of Solomon,[22] a matter of shame for

---

[16] *Hipp.* 375-382.

[17] Rom 7:15-20.

[18] Sir 6:1-3; 9:8; 23:16.

[19] Prov 6:27.

[20] Sir 23:17; Prov 9:12-18 LXX.

[21] Sir 9:3, 4, 6-7, 8-9; and 23:16-21.

[22] Sir 47:19-21.

any man. A man should never find himself in subjection to any woman, including his own wife.

Excess sexual passion, like excess consumption of wine, and especially when the two were combined, was dangerous[23] and might also lead to one using up all one's semen and becoming "a dry tree".[24] Ben Sira associates such dangers with women in general, whom he sees as the source of men's trouble in this regard. When he writes, "From a woman sin had its beginning, and because of her we all die",[25] he may be referring to Eve or to wicked women or women in general, but the message is the same; they spell danger. Concern with wicked women appears in the *Psalms of Solomon* in a prayer to be kept from seduction by attractive women.[26] The *Apocalypse of Abraham* has Eve symbolise desire,[27] and expounds desire as the head of all lawlessness.[28] Yet it is happy to have Adam and Eve entwine, since the issue with desire is not desire itself but its excess and misdirection.

It was not difficult to find stories in Israel's tradition of men whose flaw was failure to control their sexual passion, from Samson to David and Solomon. *Pseudo-Philo* highlights Samson's obsession with Delilah,[29] and Sisera's besottedness with Jael,[30] a model for Holofernes' similar demise at the hands of Judith in the legendary writing which bears her name.[31] The silly and wicked men who lust after Susanna, the corrupt judge with lustful eyes in the *Psalms of Solomon*,[32] and the spoof on woman's greatness in the *Tale of the Three Youths*, that depicts men falling captive to uncontrolled passions, serve to make the point.

Most Jewish writings which developed such themes did so under the influence of Hellenistic philosophy, especially Stoic thought, which was deemed closely compatible with Jewish ideas and traditions. The author of 4 Maccabees, writing in Greek of high style in the mid to late first century C. E., uses the martyrdom of the elderly priest, Eleazar, and of a Jewish woman and her seven sons at the hands of Antiochus, at the time of the Maccabean revolt, as a model of control and of the endurance which control makes possible. While its primary focus is the control of fear and pain through reason, it also addresses passions generally, including anger and sexual passion. Pleasure and pain are not evils, but like plants, it argues, in the

---

[23] Sir 6:1-2; 18:30 – 19:3; 26:8-9; 32:5-6.
[24] Sir 6:2.
[25] Sir 25:24.
[26] *Pss. Sol.* 16:7-8.
[27] *Apoc. Abr.* 23:10-11.
[28] *Apoc. Abr.* 24:9.
[29] *LAB* 43:5.
[30] *LAB* 31:3-7.
[31] Jdt 10 – 13.
[32] *Ps. Sol.* 4:11-12.

garden of the soul which have their proper place; they need to be kept in trim.[33] It is one of many writings which find in Joseph the model of controlling sexual passion.[34]

Control of passion is a theme in *Pseudo-Phocylides*, a set of instructions for life written in poetic style around the turn of the era masquerading as the work of the ancient Greek poet, Phocylides. Love of passion for its own sake is dangerous[35] as is unrestrained love for women.[36] *Pseudo-Aristeas*, written two centuries earlier, another pseudonymous tract, purports to have ambassadors from Jerusalem's high priest impressing Ptolemy 2 Philadelphus of Egypt with Jewish wisdom in which typically Hellenistic warnings about passions feature strongly.[37] As another work, written in the name of an ancient philosopher, the Wisdom of Solomon, asserts: "roving desire undermines an innocent mind".[38] Written in Alexandria in the early first century B. C. E., it typically merges Jewish and Hellenistic thought.

Prostitution

The audience for such exhortations are both unmarried and married men, in most instances within an educational setting in the broadest sense, where popular philosophy or life skills were taught, whether schools or communal faith gatherings, synagogues. The disparity between the ages of men and women at marriage, caused not least by the need for the former to have established themselves sufficiently to begin a new household, would mean for many that they had to deal with their natural sexual responses for at least a decade before they married. As noted in chapter 2, the expectation or ideal was that they remain chaste. Unlike their future partners, who probably for that reason were married off as young as possible, they did not face the danger of shame through becoming pregnant out of wedlock. There were models to inspire restraint, like Joseph.

For those, however, who did not refrain, the options were few. They included engaging with prostitutes, whether openly identified as such or wives surreptitiously supplementing their household income with or without their husband's knowledge. For some, prostitution was a means of survival, especially if divorced or widowed and without the normal refuge of finding support in their family of origin or from among their children. According to Philo seeking sexual

---

[33] 4 Macc 1:29.

[34] 4 Macc 2:2-3; cf. also *Jub.* 39:5-11; Wis 10:13; *T. Jos.* 3 – 9; *Asen.* 4:7; 7:3, 5; Esther C 26, 28 and Jdt 10:3-5.

[35] *Ps.-Phoc.* 67.

[36] *Ps.-Phoc.* 193-194.

[37] *Ps.-Arist.* 177, 227, 237, 256, 277-278.

[38] Wis 4:12.

experience with prostitutes was quite normal in non-Jewish society, once boys turned 14 years of age, but not at all among Jews.[39] The reality was probably that a good number of Jewish boys ignored such ideals.

It would have been safer to engage with a prostitute, as Proverbs advises, than with a married woman (acting as a prostitute), because the latter belonged to another man and so such engagement would constitute adultery, infringing her husband's rights and could have dire consequences.[40] The same would be true of intercourse with a woman still under guardianship of her father. A prostitute, not owned in this way by a man, cost little.[41] The references to prostitutes in Jewish literature including in Matthew's gospel[42] suggest their existence and their use by men in the Jewish world. It is very likely that among the "sinners" present at meals Jesus attended with tax collectors were women plying their trade.

Israel's traditions sometimes refer to prostitutes. One, Rahab, was a hero, facilitating the fall of Jericho.[43] Jacob's son, Judah, visited a prostitute, only to discover that she was his daughter-in-law trapping him into taking seriously the obligations he had to ensure his youngest son married her.[44] Judah was doubly in the wrong, but the emphasis lies on his failed obligation, not on his seeking out a prostitute. Priests were forbidden to marry prostitutes or to make their daughters prostitutes[45] – a desperate measure driven by poverty, as it still is.

The clearest condemnation of prostitution comes not in the Hebrew Bible but in its Greek translation, namely in Deut 23:17. While originally concerned with prostitution and its proceeds in relation to the temple, the text undergoes an expansion in the Greek version, which now condemns all prostitution. Its condemnation, at least for married men, is however already implied in the use of prostitute and prostitution as a metaphor to deplore Israel's engagement in idolatry.[46] Jeremiah has God condemn the people of Jerusalem for going to the houses of prostitutes and for adulterous behaviour.[47]

Prostitution is a common theme in the literature of the day. When Ben Sira warns not only against the prostitute, but also female musicians and, again, wayward married women,[48] we can recognise a common social context for

---

[39] *Ios.* 42.

[40] Prov 2:16-19; 5:3-20; 6:24-35; 7:6-27.

[41] Prov 6:26.

[42] Matt 21:31-32; cf. also Sir 9:3, 4, 6-7; 19:2; 23:16-21; 41:20; Let Jer 42-43; 2 Macc 6:3-6; *Pss. Sol.* 2:11-13; *T. Mos.* 8:3; 1 Macc 1:15; 2:46; 2 Macc 6:10; *Jub.* 15:33-34.

[43] Josh 2:1; 6:17, 23-25.

[44] Genesis 38.

[45] Lev 21:7; 19:29.

[46] Hos 9:1; Exod 34:15-16; Lev 17:7; 20:5.

[47] Jer 5:7; similarly Hos 4:14; 9:1.

[48] Sir 9:3, 4, 6-7; 19:2; 23:16-21; 41:20.

prostitution, namely feasts and parties where hired prostitutes frequently entertained in various ways. Philo frequently depicts such settings as the context for various kind of prostitution, male and female, usually accompanied by excessive consumption of alcohol.[49] The *Testaments of the Twelve Patriarchs* reflects the connection when it refers to making singing girls or prostitutes of one's daughters.[50] There appears to be an association between tax collectors and prostitutes in the gospels,[51] though no firm evidence that the former hired the latter. As noted already, the mention of "sinners" in the context of their meals may include various entertainers, among them, prostitutes.

When *Pseudo-Philo* retells the story of Judah and Tamar, it exonerates Tamar for her act of incest under the guise of being a prostitute, at least in the sense that her act was far preferable to marrying a foreigner.[52] It similarly makes no reference to Jephthah's being the son of a prostitute and so banished by his brothers,[53] but does turn Samson's Delilah into a prostitute by merging accounts of two different women[54] and so make her a stereotype of the foreign seducer who destroys foolish men.[55]

Prostitution was a common target in attacks by Jews on the world which surrounded them. Thus Book 5 of the *Sibylline Oracles* charges Rome with turning its vestal virgins into prostitutes.[56] The *Letter of Jeremiah*, written some time between the late fourth and the second century B. C. E., links prostitution to foreign cults.[57] 2 Maccabees deplores prostitution in the temple precincts.[58] Many put the presence of prostitution down to foreign influences.[59] The *Testament of Moses*, written in Greek in the late first century B. C. E. or early first century C. E., alleges that Jewish women were engaging in prostitution with foreigners.[60] The *Psalms of Solomon* similarly alleges that men were setting up their daughters as prostitutes.[61] The *Testaments of the Twelve Patriarchs* predicts that Levi's descendants, the priests, would cohort with prostitutes.[62]

---

[49] *Opif.* 158; *Spec.* 1.192-193; see also *QG* 2.12; *Somn.* 2.147; *Mos.* 2.185.

[50] *T. Jud.* 23:2.

[51] Matt 21:31-32.

[52] *LAB* 9:5.

[53] *LAB* 39:1-11; Judg 11:1.

[54] Judg 16:1, 4.

[55] *LAB* 43:5.

[56] *Sib. Or.* 5:388.

[57] Let Jer 42-43.

[58] 2 Macc 6:3-6.

[59] 1 Macc 1:15; 2:46; 2 Macc 6:10; *Jub.* 15:33-34.

[60] *T. Mos.*8:3.

[61] *Ps. Sol.* 2:11-13.

[62] *T. Levi* 14:5-6; cf. also *T. Benj.* 9:1.

There is little if any reflection on the social causes for why women might engage in prostitution. We read of men prostituting their wives and daughters, which might reflect exploitative greed or desperation.[63] We also hear of wives engaging in prostitution without their husband's knowledge,[64] creating a very dangerous situation for clients if caught, as already Proverbs notes, since adultery becomes the charge.[65] Other texts mention widows who do so[66] instead of following the model of chastity like Judith[67] and Luke's Anna.[68] This, too, might reflect poverty. Only occasionally do we hear of the abuse which such women would have endured, such as indirectly when Philo urges husbands not to treat their wives as though they were prostitutes.[69]

When Josephus insists that sexual intercourse belongs only between man and wife, he clearly sets himself against Roman norms which allowed men to engage sexually with other women under their control and with prostitutes.[70] He also employs Deut 23:18 to condemn female prostitution as outrageous and shameful.[71] Paul may well be attacking such norms in his letter to the Corinthians, where he notably uses Gen 2:24 about becoming one flesh through sexual union to argue that such sexual engagement creates a permanent relationship of oneness and so severs one's relationship with Christ.[72] The word which he uses to describe the forbidden partner *porne* was commonly used for prostitute, but could also simply mean any women with whom sex was illicit. Josephus extends to all Jews the ban in Leviticus on priests marrying former prostitutes.[73] Philo, on the other hand, argues against this, affirming that it was acceptable to marry reformed prostitutes.[74]

Confused speculation has led to the myth that Mary Magdalene was a former prostitute, but the early sources indicate no such thing. The confusion results in part from identifying the woman who anointed Jesus in Luke's version of the story with Mary,[75] which has no support in the text. She is named among women followers of Jesus in the passage which follows the anointing,[76] but is not

---

[63] *Ps.-Phoc.* 177-178.

[64] Prov 9:12-18 LXX; *Ps.-Phoc.* 177-178.

[65] Prov 6:26; similarly Sir 26:22.

[66] *Sib. Or.* 3:43-44; cf. 4QD^e/4Q270 2 i.17.

[67] Jdt 8:1-3; 16:22.

[68] Luke 2:36-37.

[69] *Spec.* 3.80.

[70] *A.J.* 4.206.

[71] *A.J.* 4.206.

[72] 1 Cor 6:16.

[73] *A.J.* 4.245; cf. Lev 21:7.

[74] *Spec.* 1.101-102.

[75] Luke 7:36-50.

[76] Luke 8:1-3.

identified with the woman who did the anointing. That woman, described as a known sinner,[77] was probably a prostitute, an assumption which may lie in the background of the different accounts in Matthew and Mark,[78] but is certainly not the case in the Gospel of John, where she is Martha's sister, Mary.[79] Perfumed massage oil will have belonged to the art of seduction, but that was not its only use.

Confronting the Dangers

A number of texts depict prostitutes or simply morally loose women as taking a very active role in setting about to seduce men. One of the best known early examples is in Proverbs where the seductress becomes a symbol of the invitation to folly (which will also have included literally falling into sexual wrongdoing as Proverbs' exhortations show). It depicts the seductive stranger as forsaking the partner of her youth,[80] so an adulteress, seducing with words smoother than oil,[81] and so posing a far greater danger than liaison with a prostitute for a loaf of bread, since it courts the vengeance of the husband and could lead to financial disaster or even to death.[82] She appears on the street, and at the squares, corners, and public places, as a loud and wayward woman, dressed like a prostitute, seizing and kissing passers-by, enticing them to a night of sex while her husband is away, snaring them into her house of death.[83] The Greek translation identifies her more clearly as a prostitute.

This woman thus represents in part what she comes to symbolise, namely the folly of flouting God's law. The author has created from the same image, however, a counter-figure, drawing on a rich mythological heritage, to speak of God's wisdom as a woman, who also lures men, not to death and destruction, but to life. She, too, "cries out in the street, in the squares she raises her voice. At the busiest corner she cries out; at the entrance of the city gates she speaks",[84] inviting people to her house and her feast.[85] Generated from the context of male preoccupation with sexual seduction we thus have two opposing symbols, Wisdom and Folly.[86]

---

[77] Luke 7:37.
[78] Mark 14:3-9; Matt 26:6-13.
[79] John 12:1-8.
[80] Prov 2:16-19.
[81] Prov 5:20; similarly 6:24.
[82] Prov 5:5, 9-10; 6:24-35.
[83] Prov 7:6-27.
[84] Prov 1:20-21; similarly 8:4-36.
[85] Prov 9:1-7.
[86] Prov 9:13-18.

Both have the effect of affirming sexual attraction, but setting it clearly in its place. We shall return to the positive implications of this below.

The image of the seductress in Proverbs inspired similar warnings in Ben Sira about the dangers of women,[87] especially prostitutes, but also about the wayward wives of others or one's own, though he does not employ the symbol of Folly, but only the symbolic application to Wisdom. Like Proverbs the *Wiles of the Wicked Woman* found at Qumran operates at both levels, the literal danger of seduction by immoral women and the woman as symbolism of Folly and lawlessness. Philo draws both on Proverbs and on Hellenistic models which used the image to depict the struggle between virtue and pleasure (in evil).[88]

Merging Greek and Jewish Wisdom on the Passions

The best known exponent of merging Greek and Jewish wisdom is Philo, in whose extensive collection of works passion is a key theme. In the first chapter we noted how Philo employs the creation stories of Genesis as a source for reflection on how to live, including how to manage passion. At times he appears to demand that passions be denied entirely, indeed, that they be excised.[89] Anger, located in the chest, should be eliminated. With the other main passions, hunger, thirst, and sexual desire, located in the abdomen, their elimination becomes problematic, as he acknowledges in depicting Moses as a model. He does have Moses embrace celibacy, but then only as an exception for a special role in the divine presence.

Despite his rhetoric and his belief that human faultiness derives from God's helpers, he cannot bring himself to deny that creation is good and that includes the passions. In the end that means: because passions are so dangerous they must be kept under careful control,[90] but they are not, in themselves, evil. To claim the latter would, as Philo acknowledges, hardly make sense in relation to hunger and thirst, and also does not make sense in relation to sexual desire, because its fulfilment in pleasure promotes the coming together which is essential for the propagation of the species. Thus Philo does not reduce sexual intercourse to a merely functional undertaking which should be devoid of pleasure, a kind of robotic insemination. It is important for him that he portrays Abraham's intercourse with the slave Hagar in this way,[91] but this stands in contrast to the way he portrays intercourse between Abraham and Sarah, which affirms their pleasure in one another.[92]

---

[87] E.g. Sir 9:1-9; 41:20.

[88] *Sacr.* 21-23; *Opif.* 166.

[89] *Leg.* 3.129

[90] *Spec.* 1.9; *Leg.* 3.118, 140, 147, 159.

[91] *Abr.* 253.

[92] *QG* 3.20-21; *Abr.* 245-246.

As noted above, Philo develops a correlation between personal self-management and household management in good Hellenistic tradition and elaborates it with great imagination. As the mind must control the emotions and passions, so in the body of the household the man must control the woman.[93] For neither the passions nor women are evil. They are simply of a lesser order and created as such and so should be kept in their place. In their place they are to be valued. Indeed, a good and fruitful relationship between mind and passions, man and woman, is to be highly valued. The model is slightly awkward because Philo knows that women also have minds and men have passions. Women do not consist entirely of passion, but, like most of his time, Philo believed that women's minds were inferior to men's and did not have the same capacity to control, including to control themselves and so needed men to exercise that role over them. In the broadest sense this is misogynist, but not so in the literal sense of hatred of women. Philo would have seen it as giving women the respect and honour they deserved.

Josephus' voluminous works frequently identify the excesses of passion, from the sexual violence especially against women in war to the stupidity of men overwhelmed by women's beauty. Rape in war of both women and men was more than opportunistic self-indulgence; it was deliberate humiliation, especially of men, reduced to the passive role of women, their virility denied. Captive men castrated to become eunuchs, also feminised, and women made available to winning men as a commodity were typical victims of war in Josephus' accounts which also reflected reality.

Josephus frequently psychologises in his accounts of sexual responses, not least in his depictions of men failing to control their passions. He, too, highlights Samson's fatal flaw as his obsession with Delilah.[94] David failed to restrain his desire in relation to Bathsheba,[95] Amnon was driven by passion in raping Tamar,[96] and Solomon was insanely enamoured and "carried away by thoughtless pleasure".[97] Time after time he portrays men failing to control themselves. He shares with Philo the view that women were not created equal, lacked control of their passions, and so presented danger, but with Philo asserted that men were therefore all the more responsible. His most tragic example of failure is Herod the Great, where probably helped by strong tendencies in his source, Nicolas of Damascus, Josephus portrays Herod as driven to mad behaviour, including the tragic murder of his own, those whom he loved, because of his unrelenting passion and jealousy.

---

[93] *Leg.* 3.220; *Her.*186; *Abr.* 109, 116.

[94] *A.J.* 5. 286, 306.

[95] *A.J.* 7.130-158.

[96] *A.J.* 7.162-180.

[97] *A.J.* 8.193.

The advice given by successive patriarchs in the *Testaments of the Twelve Patriarchs*, matches that of Philo and Josephus. Stoic psychology merges with a commitment to divine order, as expressed in biblical law.[98] The author notes that young men should have an understanding of the impact of stimuli on the senses and the processes entailed in making an appropriate response.[99] He describes the process as being like conception, one's mind falling pregnant to women's sexuality, which is sleepless until it brings its corrupt plan to birth.[100] He deals with the process of moving from hurt to anger to murder similarly in *T. Gad*. Ignorance is danger and leads a man to failure to observe "the law of God" and to departure from "the admonitions of his fathers".[101]

If anything, it is even more negative about women's capacity for self-control and so the danger they present, claiming divine revelation to justify what was nothing less than widespread popular prejudice.[102] Women allegedly cannot help themselves wanting to have sex and so do everything to achieve that goal, from adornments to trickery.[103] Tamar's seduction of Judah symbolises women's capacity to conquer even kings with their wiles[104] just as they seduced the Watchers.[105] Equipped with this knowledge one should therefore avoid their company, especially that of married women, not gaze at them so as not to be taken in by their beauty and the sexual pressure they exert.[106] Even dead drunk, as he portrays poor Bilhah, Jacob's slave, they are a threat.[107]

Naturally Joseph is the positive hero of sexual propriety. Reuben, who raped Bilhah, and Judah, who engaged in incest with Tamar, are the villains. Wine makes matters worse. It troubles the mind with "filthy thoughts" and warms the body up for sex,[108] desensitising one's sense of shame.[109] The author blames wine for both Judah's marrying the Canaanite, Bath-shua, and his falling to Tamar's seduction. Being drunk can also lead one to divulge secrets.[110] Excess is on all accounts to be avoided.

---

[98] *T. Reub.* 2:1 – 3:8.

[99] *T. Reub.* 2:1-2; 4:7.

[100] *T. Reub.* 3:12; cf. also 5:6; *T. Benj.* 7:2.

[101] *T. Reub.* 3:8; cf. *T. Jud.* 19:3-4.

[102] *T. Reub.* 5:3.

[103] *T. Reub.* 5:1-5.

[104] *T. Jud.* 15:5-6.

[105] *T. Reub.* 5:6-7.

[106] *T. Reub.* 3:10; 4:1.

[107] *T. Reub.* 3:13.

[108] *T. Jud.* 14:2-3; cf. also 16:1.

[109] *T. Jud.* 14:5.

[110] *T. Jud.* 12:6; 16:4; 18:2.

Its extreme statement that "women are evil" and like mire and dung[111] must be read within this context, rather than as a global statement which would exclude holy women, such as Rachel, who is held up as a model for seeking sexual intercourse only for procreation.[112] But in its accounts such women are few and far between. Most women apparently cannot help themselves, but men, he assures us, can, despite the uphill struggle which sometimes appears hopeless.[113] They can even find forgiveness and be rehabilitated through prayer and fasting to begin again.[114]

Out of Control

Sexual wrongdoing in Philo, Josephus, and the *Testaments of the Twelve Patriarchs*, but also in many other writings of the time, is seen as the result of losing control of one's passions. We have already discussed the prohibition of adultery, one of the ten commandments. It was often the rallying point for expositions of all kinds of other sexual wrongdoing, as it is in Philo's detailed discussions in his *De decalogo*. We have also noted incest, prostitution, and pre-marital sex in this regard.

In addition, rape, sexual penetration by force, usually by men of women, falls clearly within this category, though it was then (as it can be now) often as much about forceful humiliation as about forcing on others the fulfilment of one's sexual desires. In war it is often both. Thus it features in many of Josephus' accounts of military conquest and battle. The regulations imposing a timeline on sexual access to women taken captive[115] are a form of controlling what is in effect institutionalised rape, while not averting it. The hostility of Lot's fellow citizens expressed itself in a plan for male rape.[116] Its grotesque parallel in Judges records the terrible violence done to the Levite's concubine,[117] which might have been done to the daughters of Lot, who was willing not to spare them.[118] As noted earlier, *Pseudo-Philo* strains credibility and decency in then blaming the woman as somehow deserving because she had slept with a foreigner.[119]

---

[111] *T. Reub.* 5:1; 8:2-3.

[112] *T. Iss.* 2:1-3.

[113] *T. Reub.* 2:9; 3:8; 5:4; *T. Jud.* 11:1; 18:3, 6; 19:4; *T. Sim.* 2:7.

[114] *T. Reub.* 1:10; *T. Jud.* 15:4; 19:3-4.

[115] Deut 21:10-14.

[116] Gen 19:4-5.

[117] Judg 19:22-30.

[118] Gen 19:8.

[119] *LAB* 45:1-6.

There are many references to rape or attempted rape of women.[120] Judith confronts the possibility and likens her potential fate to Dinah,[121] whose forceful abduction is recalled also in Theodotus,[122] *Aseneth*;[123] and *Demetrius*.[124] In Judith's story Holofernes' eunuch reduces her to being a "pretty girl", ripe for his (or their) exploitation.[125] Apparently not to rape her would bring shame on Holofernes.[126] Susanna similarly faced the prospect of rape. The Greek version of Esther exposes the violence of the story, her abduction from her husband Mordecai to the harem in the hands of a eunuch, to be tried out and then be made a consort, much to her pain and disgust.[127] The conflict had begun when Vashti the queen refused to be shown off as a sex object.[128] The *Testament of Solomon* is replete with grotesque accounts of pederastic rape, including the story of Eros as the offspring of anal rape.[129]

Sometimes, however, the focus is more on the man's misdeed as wronging the woman's husband or father than it is on the woman. Thus in the *Testament of the Twelve Patriarchs*, which makes Reuben's rape of Bilhah, the basis for an exposition on sexual wrongdoing, nothing is said about how it affected Bilhah.[130] Only the men, Reuben and Jacob, whom Reuben wronged, matter. Similarly there are indications that some felt they had to blame Dinah for her abduction.[131]

Biblical law had its provisions for dealing with unauthorised sex, which may have included sex by force. They, too, show scant regard for the woman. The penalty for seizing a virgin and lying with her is payment of 50 shekels to the girl's father and the obligation to marry and never divorce her.[132] Doing so to a woman engaged to be married to another brought the death penalty to both if she was in earshot and had not cried for help,[133] but only to the man if she had.[134] Philo deals with all these provisions in his extended discussion, adding also provisions for dealing with rape of a widow or divorcee,[135] which he treats as not as serious as

---

[120] 4 Ezra 10:22; *2 Bar.* 27:11; 44:2; *T. Job* 39:1-2; *Ps.-Phoc.* 198.

[121] Jdt 9:2; 12:11-12.

[122] Theod. 4.11.

[123] *Asen.* 23:14.

[124] Demetrius 9.

[125] Jdt 12:13.

[126] Jdt 11:11-12.

[127] Esther C 24-29/14:13-18; D 7/15:7; 2:7 LXX B.

[128] Esther 1:11.

[129] *T. Sol.* 14:4.

[130] *T. Reub.* 2:11-15.

[131] *ALD* 1:1-3 / 1c 2; Theod. 4 7-9.

[132] Deut 22:28-29.

[133] Deut 22:23-24.

[134] Deut 23:25-27.

[135] *Spec.* 3.64.

adultery. As noted above his ground for disapproval of raping an unmarried woman is that it is like treating her as you do your slaves,[136] a telling exposure of what slaves must have faced. The *Testaments of the Twelve Patriarchs* alleges that Levi's corrupt priestly descendant would include rape of virgins among their crimes.[137]

Bestiality by both men and women presumably fell into the category of a crime of uncontrolled sexual passion. The prohibition in Leviticus[138] is repeated in *Ps.-Phoc.*,[139] and the practice may be in mind when the author of *2 Enoch* warns against abuse of animals.[140] It is one of the charges laid against Rome in *Sib. Or.* 5[141] and belongs to the evils of the last age according to the *Testaments of the Twelve Patriarchs.*[142] It also features among the bizarre demonic deeds in the *Testament of Solomon* where it accounts for the origin of the demon Onoskelis, who is the offspring of a man anally penetrating a donkey.[143]

Some other alleged wrongs are also attributed to failure to control passion. These include the prohibition of intercourse during pregnancy, as propounded by Josephus,[144] the *Damascus Document*,[145] and assumed in the *Genesis Apocryphon*. The latter depicts Lamech's consternation over the baby Noah's beauty and suspects that Bitenosh his wife must have consorted with a Watcher. She protests,[146] recalling for Lamech their intensely pleasurable act of intercourse through which Noah will have been conceived.[147] The assumption is that this was the last time that they had had intercourse and that they had abstained throughout the pregnancy. While not opposing intercourse during pregnancy, Philo, like many others of his time, saw engagement in sexual intercourse just for pleasure as a sign of uncontrolled passion, as we have seen above. In fact, a number of other prohibitions, which have different origins, such as not having sex during menstruation, would have been deemed to occur when men allowed their passions to get the better of them. An extreme stance would be to argue that wasting seed, that is ejaculation in any other context than for propagation of the species with one's spouse, illustrated failure to control passions, certainly ruling out all sex with

---

[136] *Spec.* 3.69.

[137] *T. Levi* 14:6.

[138] Lev 18:23.

[139] *Ps.-Phoc.*188.

[140] *2 Enoch* 59:5; 58:6.

[141] *Sib. Or.* 5:387-396.

[142] *T. Levi* 17:11.

[143] *T. Sol.* 4:1-2.

[144] *B.J.* 2.161.

[145] 4QD^e/4Q270 2 ii.15-16; 6QD/6Q15 5 2-3; 4QD^b/4Q267 9 vi.4-5.

[146] 1QapGen ar/1Q20 2.1.

[147] 1QapGen ar/1Q20 2.9-10.

others, women or men or animals, all sex outside fertile years or fertile days, all non-vaginal sex, including anal and *fellatio*,[148] *coitus interruptus*,[149] and masturbation. As we have seen, while Philo might have generally agreed, he could still embrace exceptions where sexual relations belonged to the intimacy of a continuing but infertile marriage.[150]

Generally, most if not all Jews embraced what they saw as useful and compatible in Hellenistic philosophy within the framework of the presupposition that human beings, men and women, mind and passions, were God's creation. Things went wrong when any of these got out of control, which resulted in their functioning in ways which perverted God's original intention. This certainly applied to sexual passion. It was not something evil in itself. The same assumptions inform treatment of passion and desire in the writings of the New Testament, in particular in those which do more than simply list the evils to which passions can lead. Paul's treatment of sexual desire, who has most to say on the matter, is no exception. He warns against enflamed passion and the perversions to which it leads, as we shall see below, and recommends that people refrain from acting out their passions in relation to proceeding to marriage if they can, his own preference, but defends those for whom this is not a realistic option, reassuring them that sexual passion is not something bad. It has its place in mutual intimacy in marriage.

Eunuchs

Eunuchs were an anomaly. In some texts the word, eunuch, seems to have meant a royal or governmental official and nothing more. Thus Joseph's master, Potiphar, is described in *Jubilees* as Pharaoh's eunuch, though he was a married man with children, one of whom, Aseneth, Joseph married.[151] This broader usage will have developed from the fact that many employed to serve in the courts of rulers were in fact eunuchs, castrated, but then the term came by extension to refer to all such servants. A saying attributed to Jesus describes three categories of eunuch: those who are infertile and were born that way; those who have been castrated or emasculated and so rendered impotent; and those who voluntarily choose not to engage in sexual intercourse, not to marry.[152] The last is a metaphorical innovation, though some like Origen later took it literally, undergoing castration, a practice against which the later councils of the church had to issue a decree.

---

[148] Possibly *Sib. Or.* 5:392.

[149] *LAB* 9:4; *T. Jud.* 10:4-5.

[150] *Spec.* 3.35.

[151] *Jub.* 39:2; 40:10-11; cf. Gen 39:1; 41:45.

[152] Matt 19:12.

In our period most references to eunuchs are to those literally castrated and so rendered impotent. Deuteronomy 23 declares them banned from joining the assembly of God's people: "No one whose testicles are crushed or whose penis is cut off shall be admitted to the assembly of the LORD."[153] They are excluded, along with those born out of illicit sexual relations, the *mamzer*, though the latter's descendants may enter after ten generations. In neither are the people themselves to blame, but they are the product of what ought not to be according to the Law.

Castrating males, like rape, was an instrument of subjugation in the context of war and conquest, as Josephus records.[154] Masters might castrate male slaves and most eunuchs serving rulers will have suffered the same fate. It was a crude way of ensuring that one could have male help close at hand in the household without being in danger that such men might make female members pregnant. Jewish law prohibited castration, as the ban expressed in Deuteronomy 23 makes clear.[155] The author of *Pseudo-Phocylides* strongly condemns it.[156] The Roman emperor, Domitian, forbade it by the imperial edict, *Lex Cornelia de sicariis et veneficis*.[157]

Despite the voices of disapproval, formal and otherwise, eunuchs were not an unfamiliar phenomenon in the world of the time and so feature in Jewish and early Christian literature. Sometimes they are simply part of the state apparatus, where they may or may not be literally eunuchs, though most presumably were. Josephus refers to such court servants in his accounts,[158] including some in highly influential positions.[159] The Ethiopian eunuch mentioned in Acts is probably such a court official.[160]

While one might suppose that eunuchs were by nature deprived of their sexual impulses and so of only negative relevance for our discussions, this is far from the case. Being impotent did not mean being without sexual desire. Ben Sira likens impotent idols and people doing good under compulsion to frustrated eunuchs, who desire to violate virgins, embrace them and then groan.[161] The legend of Judith may well imply that not only Holofernes, but also his eunuch, Bagoas, looked forward to sexually violating Judith.[162] Philo sees eunuchs as far from innocent victims rendered impotent,[163] but rather as often sexually self-indulgent

---

[153] Deut 23:1.

[154] *A.J.* 10.33.

[155] Philo *Ebr.* 211-212; Josephus *A.J.* 4.290-291.

[156] *Ps.-Phoc.* 187.

[157] Suetonius *Dom.* 7.1.

[158] E.g. *A.J.* 8.403.

[159] *A.J.* 9.122; 10.149; 11.200.

[160] Acts 8:27.

[161] Sir 20:4; 30:19-20.

[162] Jdt 12:11, 13.

[163] *Ios.* 58.

and perverse.[164] They are for him a symbol of subversion and seduction.[165] The author of Wisdom speaks of their hands as instruments of wrongdoing, probably referring to manual stimulation or masturbation, presumably of others.[166] Such behaviour might have belonged to the repertoire of eunuchs placed in charge of harems, such as the eunuch in charge of the harem in Esther's story,[167] and be part of preparing their charges for their plight.

Josephus allows us to see that Herod's eunuchs, who put him to bed, had a sexual role, which Alexander, his son, exploited to shame his father, by paying to have sex with them and do to Herod what Absalom had done to his father David, by sleeping with his concubines.[168]

At another level, most had been clearly victims of violence and some, impotent from birth. Sensitivity to their plight probably inspired the prophet among the deported Jews in Babylon, whose oracles have been incorporated into the book of Isaiah. As they predict that the temple would become "a house of prayer for all peoples", cited in Jesus' dramatic last act in the temple,[169] so also they promise that there will be a place of honour for eunuchs and Gentiles, provided they keep the sabbath: "Do not let the foreigner joined to the LORD say, 'The LORD will surely separate me from his people'; and do not let the eunuch say, 'I am just a dry tree'."[170] Perhaps it reflects a situation where many Jewish male captives had been castrated by their captors, as one source predicted.[171] The book of Wisdom alludes to this passage from Isaiah in promising hope for eunuchs.[172] Significantly it couples the promise with hope for infertile women, based on the same prophet.[173] Far from being shamed and accursed,[174] they will bear fruit, if they have not exploited their condition to engage in illicit sex.[175]

The Flesh

There are some instances, however, where what appear to be derogatory comments about the human constitution might suggest that authors see flesh and blood,

---

[164] *Mut.* 173; *Somn.* 2.184; *Deus* 111.

[165] *Ios.* 63.

[166] Wis 3:14.

[167] Esther 2:8 LXXB.

[168] *A.J.* 16.229-231; *B.J.* 1.488-492.

[169] Mark 11:17; cf. Isa 56:7.

[170] Isa 65:3-8.

[171] 2 Kgs 20:18.

[172] Wis 3:14.

[173] Isa 54:1.

[174] Cf. Gen 30:23; Judg 13:2; Job 15:34; Isa. 4:1; *1 Enoch* 98:5; Luke 1:25.

[175] Wis 3:13.

including sexuality, as evil, as some from later times would. One particular instance is found in descriptions of creatureliness in documents found at Qumran. In the *Thanksgiving Scroll*, especially, we have such statements, with some parallels also in the hymn with which the *Community Rule* concludes and elsewhere.[176] At times they serve as a contrast in order to praise God's greatness and goodness and so evoke wonder and thanksgiving. At times they emphasise human frailty. Typically the authors refer to the substances which according to the creation story in Genesis 2 make up the human being: dust, dirt, earth, and by derivation, mixed with water: clay. Sometimes the word, "flesh", is used in this sense and sometimes in addition we find reference to mere spit, an allusion to semen. Nowhere do we find the implication that any of these substances or the processes with which they are associated, such as sexual intercourse, are bad or evil. They are simply illustrative of the lowliness of human beings.

To that lowliness belongs the need regularly to undergo purification. Their excretions make human beings ritually "dirty", which at one level brings shame, though not guilt as though creatureliness is sin. Those impurities have a lot to do with sex. The penis is described for instance as "source/spring of impurity",[177] but neither impurities nor sexual genitalia are seen as sin.

Sin does however feature in some descriptions of human creatureliness because of what is deemed to be a propensity for humans to sin, an evil tendency. One author laments that this has been so since even before we were born, taking up the pious rhetoric of the psalms.[178] This should caution us against turning such a statement into more than that, such as one of innate sinfulness. When the authors talk in this way, they do not focus on particular parts of the human body, let alone genitalia. Rather they are referring to what is part of the human condition with the belief that God can deal with it.

Occasionally authors speak as though God has implanted the tendency or set the balance between good and evil forces within people, as we find in *Treatise on the Two Spirits*, which speaks of God's knowing and determining the inclination of every creature.[179] Yet, typically, such claims stand beside affirmations that people can choose to change. We find a similar paradox in the book of *Instruction*, which contrasts "people of the spirit" and others as belonging to the "spirit of flesh",[180] but then, however, assumes it is possible to leave one to join the other. It prefers "flesh" when designating human beings who have turned away from God. Some writers locate "the innards of the flesh" as a kind of battleground[181] against

---

[176] 4QpapRitPur B/4Q512; 4QprFêtes[a,b]/4Q507, 508.

[177] 1QH[a] ix.22; xx.25.

[178] Psalm 51:5; 1QH[a] xii.29-30; cf. also 4QPrFêtes[a]/4Q507 1.2-3.

[179] 1QS/1Q28 3.15-16; 4.16, 25-26; *4QHoroscope*/4Q186.

[180] 4QInstr[c]/4Q417 1 i.16b-18a.

[181] 4QShir[a,b]/4Q510, 511; 1QS/1Q28 4.20b-21a; *1QHymnic Composition*/1Q36 14 2.

the "bastard" spirits, who descended from the Watchers[182] and seek to entice to evil.[183] But the battleground itself is not evil or sinful.

None of these discussions focuses on human sexuality and altogether the *Thanksgiving Scroll* shows no interest in sexual sins. Others which speak of change sometimes list sexual wrongdoing among things from which God has delivered them, such as a "heart of stone", the "evil inclination", "sexual immorality of the eyes", "stiffness of neck", "wrathful anger", "haughtiness of heart and arrogance of eyes", and a "spirit of deceit".[184] In none of the documents is being flesh and being made up of all its creaturely components something sinful. And certainly human sexuality, while a source of impurities, is not a source of sin, unless wrongly directed.

The same is basically true of Paul's use of "flesh". Flesh, in itself, is not evil or sinful, but like the author of the book of *Instruction*, he often uses "flesh" in relation to people who live only by its impulses and do not allow themselves to place them within the control of the Spirit. To walk according to the flesh, for Paul, is to abdicate control and simply follow one's passions, wherever they lead, instead of walking according to the Spirit, in which case they come to serve their true purpose.[185] The passions, the natural human desires, are not evil. Right or wrong depends on how they are directed. Sexual passion uncontrolled which leads to engagement with prostitutes is a surrender of power and control.[186] Sexual passion directed to marriage is affirmed as God's intent.[187] But Paul's statements about "flesh", like those of the author of the book of *Instruction*, are not primarily focused on sex. We see this if we peruse the list of the "works of the flesh" in Galatians: "sexual wrongdoing, impurity, licentiousness, idolatry, sorcery, enmities, strife, jealousy, anger, quarrels, dissensions, factions, envy, drunkenness, carousing, and things like these".[188] Certainly sexual wrongdoing tops the list,[189] matching its importance in Paul's day and its position as first on the second table of the ten commandments in the Greek version, but the "works of the flesh" encompass much more, including behaviours which have little directly to do with physical embodiment.

---

[182] *1 Enoch* 15:8-9; 19:1.

[183] 4QShir^b/4Q511 48-49+51 ii.2b-4; similarly *4QIncantation*/ 4Q444 1-4 i +5 3; 11QapocPs/11Q11 5.6.

[184] *4QBarkhi Nafshi*/4Q434-438.

[185] Gal 5:16-25; Rom 8:1-8.

[186] 1 Cor 6:12, 14-17.

[187] 1 Cor 7:2-4, 9, 27-28, 36.

[188] Gal 5:18-20.

[189] Similarly in 1 Cor 6:9-10.

Celebrating Sexuality

It is important to note that sexual desire, including sexual attractiveness and erotic response, can also be the subject of celebration, including by those given to warning of its dangers. Philo, as we have noted, emphasises the role of pleasure in propagation. He also makes extensive use of the metaphor of sexual intercourse to describe key relationships and how they should work or have worked, including God and creation; God and wisdom; wisdom and humankind; the soul and the passions. While employment of erotic imagery need not indicate a positive attitude towards the erotic in reality, in Philo's case this seems to be so.

It is true also of the tradition of depicting Wisdom as a woman, beginning with the daring imagery in Proverbs, which creates a counterpoint to the seducer, the strange woman, Folly, who may be understood as an adulteress, a prostitute, or both, as noted above. The contrasting figure is Wisdom, who similarly sets out to lure men into an intimate relationship with herself, often depicted in erotic language.

This is especially so in Ben Sira who exploits the image extensively to depict the call of Wisdom, which, he explains, is really a call to embrace God's holy law. She invites the obedient into her secret chambers,[190] invites people to sow and plough in her field,[191] sexual imagery, and to hold her and not let her go.[192] Even more directly erotic are the images of peeping through her window;[193] listening at her doors; encamping by her house; being met by her as a young bride, who also offers bread and water,[194] a reworking of imagery in Proverbs;[195] building one's nest in her foliage and spending the night in her branches;[196] and driving one's tent peg into her wall.[197] In particular the acrostic poem in Sirach 51 is replete with erotic symbolism, where the author writes of seeking her as a young man, meeting her in her beauty, opening her gate, spending the night with her.[198] Rather than representing a sublimation of the erotic, the erotic is thereby affirmed, provided it finds its place in the divine order set by God in creation, which is in marriage, something Ben Sira affirms. The image of Wisdom as a woman is sustained also in the book of Wisdom.[199]

---

[190] Sir 4:15.
[191] Sir 6:19.
[192] Sir 6:27.
[193] Cant 2:9.
[194] Cf. Sir 24:16-22; 51:23-24.
[195] Prov 9:1-6.
[196] Sir 14:26; cf. Cant 7:6-9.
[197] Sir 14:23-26.
[198] Sir 51:13-20.
[199] cf. also *1 Enoch* 42:1-3; Bar 3:9-37; 4:1.

Thus for all the warnings and fears which Ben Sira has about the deceptions of beauty in a woman,[200] especially another's,[201] but even one's own,[202] he can affirm sexual attractiveness,[203] likening a wife's beauty to the beautiful sacred objects in the temple,[204] and as the source of life's greatest pleasure.[205] When he speaks of wounds of the heart, Ben Sira reflects emotional engagement.[206] A devoted wife surpasses all other possessions including friendships.[207]

In chapter two we noted numerous examples of the affirmation of love between men and women, including its erotic expression, from *Jubilees'* rewriting of Genesis 2 to the romance, *Joseph and Aseneth*. *Jubilees* not only affirms the sexual union between the first couple, but also portrays relationships between Abraham and Sarah, Isaac and Rebecca, and Jacob and Rachel and then Leah, as loving and affectionate. The erotic was probably present in the entertainment which *Pseudo-Aristeas* assumes and affirms, as long as it is "done with decency and moderation".[208]

The author of Tobit may playfully reflect such affirmation when he has Raguel's model wife called Edna, a word which can mean "sexual pleasure", as in Gen 18:12. In Tobias and Sarah's wedding night the emphasis lies not on procreation but on the oneness depicted in Gen 2:24.[209] In *Pseudo-Philo* Hannah defies her rival's insults about her sterility with the assertion that wealth consisted not in many offspring but in doing the will of God and engaging in sexual intimacy with her husband.[210]

The *Genesis Apocryphon* writes lyrically of Sarah's beauty: her face, her hair, her eyes, her nose, her radiance, her breasts, her whiteness, her arms, her hands, her palms, her fingers, her feet, her legs![211] "There are no virgins or brides who enter a bridal chamber more beautiful than she".[212] It was something positive even though it exposed her to danger.

Similarly Judith, like Jael trapping Sisera, deliberately presented herself as attractive, sufficient to have Holofernes' troops swoon and to bring their master to

---

[200] Sir 25:21; 26:9.

[201] Sir 9:8.

[202] Sir 25:21.

[203] Sir 26:1-4, 13-18.

[204] Sir 26:16-18.

[205] Sir 36:22-24.

[206] Sir 25:13.

[207] Sir 40:19, 23,

[208] *Ps.-Arist.* 284-287.

[209] Tob 8:6-8.

[210] *LAB* 50:1-5.

[211] 1QapGen ar/1Q20 20.2-6.

[212] 1QapGen ar/1Q20 20.6.

his end.[213]   Whether Susanna's beauty[214] or that of women generally, which according to the *Tale of the Three Youths* drives men to madness or makes Darius look a fool for his indulgence of his concubine,[215] sexual attractiveness is seen as something positive in itself. Such silliness by men is reflected in Antiochus' lavish gift of cities to his concubine[216] and in Antipas' intoxication with Herodias' daughter, which according to Mark led to the execution of John the Baptist.[217] Finding its fulfilment in marriage, sexual attractiveness was affirmed; otherwise directed it was seen as spelling disaster.

Josephus, who rails constantly against excess and misdirected passion, can nevertheless also affirm the erotic in the right place and time. The romantic, he knew, would titillate his Roman hearers, and at times he acknowledges taking a leaf out of popular romances to portray his lovers.[218] Such is the case in his depiction of the love between Herod and Mariamme at its best.[219] Like the author of the *Genesis Apocryphon*, he makes a point of highlighting Sarah's beauty as a reason for the Egyptians' inappropriate response.[220] Similarly he notes Rachel's beauty and Rachel and Jacob's falling in love.[221] The Ethiopian princess falls in love with Moses;[222] the Levite is in love with his wife (no longer depicted as his concubine),[223] as is Samson's father, Manoah, with his,[224] and Ahasuerus with Vashti.[225]

Sometimes falling in love happened where it should not have, such as when Herod's brother, Pheroras fell in love with his slave,[226] Ptolemy Chalcis fell in love with his son's wife,[227] or Mundus fell in love with Paulina.[228] The sexual response in itself is not condemned; it was a matter of directing it appropriately. Thus Joseph urges Potiphar's wife to find sexual enjoyment with her husband, not with him.[229]

---

[213] Judith 12 – 13.

[214] Sus 2.

[215] 1 Esdr 4:31.

[216] 2 Macc 4:30.

[217] Mark 6:22.

[218] *A.J.* 15.218.

[219] *A.J.* 15.82-84, 218, 240; *B.J.* 1.436.

[220] *A.J. 1.*162, 163.

[221] *A.J.* 1.291, 318.

[222] *A.J.* 2.252.

[223] *A.J.* 5.136.

[224] *A.J.* 5.276-277.

[225] *A.J.* 11.195.

[226] *A.J.* 16.194.

[227] *A.J.* 14.126.

[228] *A.J.* 18.65-80.

[229] *A.J.* 2.51-52.

Like Philo, Josephus merges affirmation of sexual pleasure with affirmation of the role of sexual intercourse as propagation. Accordingly, Adam, was "seized with a passionate desire to beget a family".[230] Passion and begetting belonged together.

The erotic scenes of the Song of Solomon inspired affirmations of sexual love, such as in the romance about *Joseph and Aseneth*, where the author describes her breasts as standing up like apples when Joseph places his hand between them.[231] Aseneth is simply beautiful.[232] Aseneth falls in love as does Joseph. They engage in sustained kissing and embracing.[233] This is romantic entertainment, patterned on Hellenistic models of the day, but also a perfect setting for its agenda of affirming marriage to proselytes.

The very negative stance taken towards sexual passion in the *Testament of the Twelve Patriarchs* also happens to co-exist with one of the most positive affirmations of sexual intimacy one could find. The patriarch Naphtali instructs his descendants to see sexual intercourse with one's wife as an expression of the second commandment, loving one's neighbour.[234] It should never usurp first place, so that times of prayer may require abstinence from intercourse, as in Paul's advice to the Corinthians,[235] but in its place it belongs to something divinely commanded and blessed. In contrast to much else in the book, the purpose of such engagement is love. There is no mention of what would also have been in the background, namely procreation.

Attacking "Perversion"

The engagement with Hellenistic culture accounts for Jewish writers giving much greater emphasis to passions and to procreation as the purpose of sexual intercourse, as they appropriated what they saw as commonly shared concerns. That engagement also accounts for increased attention to what it saw as abuses. Idolatry had always been an issue at the interface of cultures. It was frequently associated with sexual wrongdoing. Thus the prohibitions of incest and other acts of sexual wrongdoing in Leviticus 18 are prefaced by the exhortation to the Israelites: "You shall not do as they do in the land of Egypt, where you lived, and you shall not do as they do in the land of Canaan".[236] Such doings included various forms of incest as well as intercourse during menstruation; adultery; sacrificing

---

[230] *A.J.* 1.67.

[231] *Asen.* 8:8.

[232] *Asen* 18:9.

[233] *Asen* 19:11; 20:1.

[234] *T. Naph.* 8:7-10.

[235] 1 Cor 7:5.

[236] Lev 18:3.

offspring to Molech; lying "with a male as with a woman", similarly condemned, and as a capital offence in 20:13; and having sexual relations with an animal (applicable to both men and women).[237]

Same-sex intercourse took on particular significance because of its prevalence, at least in the Jewish mind, among other peoples of the period. It is absent from Ben Sira, and barely mentioned in literature emanating from the Jewish context of Judea. In the *Damascus Document* the prohibition occurs in its catalogue of transgressions[238] and it extends the prohibition of cross-dressing in Deuteronomy[239] to apply to both the outer- and the undergarment and perhaps also to unisex clothing.[240]

Issues with same-sex intercourse feature significantly, however, in writings composed where Hellenistic influence was strong. This is so in the *Sibylline Oracles*. In the earliest layer of Book 3, written in the second century B. C. E., the author attacks Rome for supporting male prostitution of boys,[241] but then extends the accusation to all nations.[242] Such behaviour, it alleges, breaches universal law.[243] The attacks on pederasty continue in Book 4, written in the first century C. E.,[244] and in book 5 from the early second century C. E.

2 Enoch, probably written at the turn of the era, similarly deplores "sin which is against nature, which is child corruption in the anus in the manner of Sodom",[245] but also "abominable fornications, that is, friend with friend in the anus, and every other kind of wicked uncleanness which it is disgusting to report".[246] Here the concern extends beyond pederasty to adult consensual same-sex relations. The latter receives attention in the late first century C. E. *Apocalypse of Abraham*, which portrays men not in anal intercourse, but standing naked forehead to forehead.[247]

Pseudo-Aristeas rails against the practice of procuring males in the cities of his world as perversion like incest.[248] The Book of Wisdom appears to make a link between having perverted ideas of God leading to idolatry and having perverted

---

[237] Lev 18:23; 20:15-16; Exod 22:19; Deut 27:21.

[238] 4QD^e/4Q270 2 ii.16b-17a / 6QD/6Q15 5 3-4.

[239] Deut 22:5.

[240] 4QD^f/4Q271 3 3-4; 4QOrd^a/ 4Q159.

[241] *Sib. Or.* 3:185-187.

[242] *Sib. Or.*3:596-599.

[243] *Sib. Or.* 3:758.

[244] *Sib. Or.* 4:33-34.

[245] *2 Enoch* 10:2.

[246] *2 Enoch* 34:1-2.

[247] *Apoc. Abr.* 24:8.

[248] *Ps.-Arist.* 152.

sexual relations.[249] The link between idolatry and sexual wrongdoing was common. The *Testaments of the Twelve Patriarchs* in linking sexual immorality and idolatry, sometimes sees the former leading to the latter,[250] sometimes the reverse.[251] The nexus between perverted understandings of God and perverted sexual behaviour, present in Wisdom, inspired the same connection made by Paul in Romans 1.

In its list of forbidden acts, citing the ten commandments, *Pseudo-Phocylides* appends to the prohibition of adultery: arousing homosexual passion.[252] In another place it takes up Plato's argument in *Laws* that animals never engage in such sexual activity,[253] repeated also by Josephus (but as we now know factually incorrect). It also deplores same-sex relations between women,[254] generally deemed unnatural and offensive[255] and advises parents to be very careful not to braid their sons' hair, lest effeminate appearance attract male sexual predators.[256] The *Testament of Solomon* portrays same-sex intercourse as something practised and inspired by the demonic. The demon Ornias rapes boys.[257] The demon Onoskelis perverts men's natures.[258] The demon Beelzeboul promotes male anal sex.[259]

The account in Genesis 19 of the men of Sodom wanting to rape Lot's male guests made the story a prime example of inhospitality. Sometimes authors focus entirely on the inhospitality with no reference to its sexual violence. Such is the case in Ben Sira[260] and Wisdom,[261] and may well be so in Luke.[262] It seems to have been the focus also earlier in Isaiah,[263] Jeremiah,[264] and Ezekiel.[265] *Jubilees* refers to sexual sin at Sodom, but without referring specifically to same-sex intercourse.[266] Among the previously unknown documents found among the Dead

---

[249] Wis 14:12.

[250] *T. Reub.* 4:6; *T. Sim.* 5:3; *T. Jud.* 23:2; cf. also *T. Dan* 5:5; *T. Benj.* 10:10.

[251] *T. Naph.* 2:2 – 3:5.

[252] *Ps.-Phoc.* 3.

[253] Plato *Leg.* 836C.

[254] *Ps.-Phoc.*190-192.

[255] Ovid *Met.* 9.728-734.

[256] *Ps.-Phoc.* 210-214.

[257] *T. Sol.* 2:3.

[258] *T. Sol.* 4:5.

[259] *T. Sol.* 6:4 MS P.

[260] Sir 16:8.

[261] Wis 10:6-8; 19:13-17.

[262] Luke 19:10-12.

[263] Isa 1:10; 3:9.

[264] Jer 23:14.

[265] Ezek 16:48-50.

[266] *Jub.* 13:13-18.

Sea Scrolls only two make brief reference to the story, one, generally with reference to sexual sin;[267] the other, speaking of disgusting acts, of spending the night together and wallowing.[268] *Pseudo-Philo* makes a connection between the intended violence at Sodom and the sexual violence against the Levite's concubine at Gibeah,[269] as does Theodotus with Dinah's abduction,[270] and possibly *2 Baruch* in depicting Manasseh's Jerusalem as like Sodom, as a place of sexual violence against women.[271]

As one might expect, Philo has much to say about same-sex intercourse. He reads the prohibitions in Lev 18:22 and 20:13 as targeting both pederasty and adult consensual sex, both male and female.[272] Apart from citing the prohibitions, he frequently gives reasons for them. Thus such behaviour wastes semen, an argument made already by Plato.[273] It also entails, at least in male-male intercourse, having a man behave as a woman. This is something much more serious than simply a role reversal. It is a step down the ladder. It renders one man inferior. It humiliates, whether by force – as in war, or consensually. That in turn, he argues, infects a man with what Philo describes as the disease of effemination, which will eventually render men impotent and so unable to fulfil the role God has given them.[274] To waste seed, to behave or cause others to behave as women, to engage in sex other than for propagation, is to act contrary to nature.

His account of Sodom portrays the men as controlled by sexual passion, leading them into promiscuity with both women and men.[275] Philo sees such behaviour typifying drunken parties of his day, where men have indiscriminate sex, often with young adolescent boy slaves conscripted or assigned to attend their needs.[276] He ridicules therefore not only Aristophanes' myth of sexual origins, which traces homosexual passion in men and women and heterosexual passion to a desire to restore original unities, which once existed when there were three kinds of human being: male, female, and bisexual, sundered in half by Zeus in a fit of rage.[277] He also scorns the symposium itself. For in such settings the combination of wine and lack of control let such passions loose.

---

[267] 4QUniden/4Q172.

[268] *4QCatena*[a]/4Q177 iv.9-10a; par. 4QBéat/4Q525 22.

[269] *LAB* 45:1-6.

[270] Theod. 7; similarly *T. Levi* 6:8-11.

[271] *2 Bar* 64:2; cf. Sodom in *Liv. Pro.* 3:6-9.

[272] *Spec.* 3.37-42; *QG* 2.49; *Virt.* 20-21; *Her.* 274.

[273] *Spec.* 3.32-33, 37, 39; *Anim.* 49; *Abr.* 135, 137; *Contempl.* 62; Plato, *Leg.* 838E-839A.

[274] *Spec.* 3.37; *Abr.* 136; *Contempl.* 60; *Plant.* 158; *Spec.* 1.325; 2.50.

[275] *Abr.* 133-141.

[276] *Abr.* 133-135; *Contempl.* 50-58; *Ebr.* 21; *Legat.* 14; *Spec.* 3.37, 40.

[277] *Contempl.* 50-63; cf. Plato *Symposium* 189-193.

It was not that at some point some men (or women) made a decision to seek out their own for sexual pleasure, as if this were a rational decision about sexual orientation or sexual preference. Rather, unbridled passion went for every fulfilment it could find, in the process producing both transgression and perversion. Philo shows no sign of contemplating that some people in sober reality might have a sexual orientation towards their own kind. The extant evidence suggests that he shared the view of all others Jews we know of from the time, namely that there are two kinds of human being, male and female, as Genesis depicts creation,[278] and anything else is a deliberate denial and perversion of that reality.

Josephus similarly views same-sex intercourse as a perversion, the fruit of uncontrolled sexual passion, also usually associated with people who were at the same time promiscuous with women. His view is clear about the role of sexual intercourse: it is "the natural union of man and wife (woman), and that, only for the procreation of children".[279] All else is perversion and abhorrent, and shames men into behaving as women. Thus he tells how Antony wanted to have both Mariamme, Herod's new wife, and her brother, Aristobulus, both apparently very attractive, come to him in Alexandria that he might engage in sex with them.[280] Deft manipulation on Herod's part rescued them from Antony's sexual intentions. For while Antony backed down on Mariamme, Herod could only save Aristobulus by appointing him high priest, contrary to his intent, which would make it illegal for him to leave the land. Herod later saved himself from the danger that created of having a high priest of the old Hasmonean line, by engineering that he drowned in a palace pool at Jericho.[281]

Machinations in Herod's household, of which there were many, including those connected with sexual issues, resulted, as noted above, in his son, Alexander, sleeping with Herod's eunuchs, much as Absalom had done with David's concubines and Abner with Saul's.[282] Thereafter these eunuchs, of whom, Josephus tells us, he was "immoderately fond ... because of their beauty", could no longer be "putting the king to bed".[283] Josephus motivates the attempted male sexual assault at Sodom as a response to what he describes as their beauty.[284] His account of David and Jonathan's love[285] gives no indication that he saw it as

---

[278] Gen 1:27.

[279] *Ap.* 2.199.

[280] *A.J.* 15.25, 30.

[281] *A.J.* 15.50-56.

[282] *A.J.* 16.230.

[283] *A.J.* 16.230.

[284] *A.J.* 1.200.

[285] *A.J.* 6.206, 241, 275; 7.5, 111.

having a sexual component, despite the use of sexual imagery in David's lament.[286] None of his contemporaries saw it that way either.

He alleged that the Zealots, who featured in the revolt against Rome which led to the fall of Jerusalem, engaged in violation of women and effeminacy, cross-dressing, and copying women's passions.[287] This probably had more to do with his agenda to denigrate the Jewish rebels before his Roman audiences and commend his own worthiness than to do with history. For Josephus knew he could find common ground with many in attacking such excesses, including in Rome, and so also deplores the "unnatural and extremely licentious intercourse with males" characteristic of Sparta, Elis and Thebes.[288]

Officially Roman law deemed same-sex intercourse among citizens as *stuprum*, a criminal act. It was depicted by many as a "Greek disease", though in reality where in Greek tradition same-sex intercourse was tolerated, it assumed relations between an older and younger male and that these would cease once the young man reached maturity. The Romans on the other hand tolerated same-sex intercourse with non-citizens of all ages, and depicted it unabashedly on their pottery and in public art, something Greeks found deplorable. Greek *kinaedos*, indicating a man who preferred to be penetrated anally, became Latin *cinaedus*, referring to someone engaged in a range of effeminate behaviours. Fantasy about lesbian relations created the bizarre fantasy of the *tribas* as a woman with a clitoris so large that it could function as a penis.

The authors of the *Sibylline Oracles* books cited above, represent the Roman scene well; brothels, with male and female prostitutes, abounded.[289] Thus Josephus might hope for a sympathetic audience among those Romans who abhorred such practices, saw them as demeaning and subverting the ideal image of the strong, disciplined male, and charged philosophers who had such close relations with their students, with hypocrisy.

As might be expected, the author of the *Testaments of the Twelve Patriarchs*, makes it clear that same-sex intercourse, which it illustrates by reference to Sodom, is a deliberate act of perversion of one's nature comparable to that of the Watchers who transgressed divine order when they engaged in sex with human women.[290] While at one point depicted primarily as a breach of hospitality and violence,[291] elsewhere it depicts the sin of Sodom and Gomorrah as illicit sexual

---

[286] 2 Sam 1:26.

[287] *B.J.* 4.561-562.

[288] *Ap.* 2.273-275.

[289] *Sib. Or.* 3:185-187; 5:386-396.

[290] *T. Naph.* 3:4-5; 4:1; see also *T. Levi* 14:6; *T. Benj.* 9:1.

[291] *T. Ash.* 7:1.

union, in the form of adult male to male sexual acts.[292] Pederasty also belongs to the evils of the last age.[293]

The mix of reasons for rejecting same-sex intercourse included, therefore, the feminisation of men, a matter of great shame; the perversion of the act, producing sperm which could not fulfil its function of procreation; manifest failure to control strong passion, resulting in connections contrary to what is natural; and, especially for Jews, flouting of both divine commandment prohibiting such acts, and the divine order which required male to mate with female and not otherwise.

These values almost certainly inform the brief reference to same-sex intercourse in Paul's letter to the Romans.[294] He could probably rely, as Josephus did, on finding willing support in his Roman audience, not least because they were mainly Jews and converts to Judaism, having to live with Rome's excesses. Even though his purpose is to use this common ground as a basis for launching into an argument that in fact all humanity stands condemned and needs redemption, his exposition of same-sex intercourse is meant to be taken with utmost seriousness.

Perversion is a key theme, probably borrowed in part from the Book of Wisdom. Accordingly, failing to comprehend God's true nature had the effect that people developed a perverted understanding also of their own selves.[295] Paul sees this not as a calm intellectual process, but as something driven by passion. Three times, using different words, he addresses passion, finally depicting is as aflame.[296] Passion aflame produces perversion. Paul no more sees this as an excuse than do his Jewish contemporaries. This is not about natural orientation into which people might have been born or which they might have developed in the processes of maturation. This is the fruit of strong passion taking over.

Though he does not say it, he may well have in mind what his contemporaries railed against: parties where drunk men engaged in promiscuous sex in all directions. He may have had boy prostitutes in mind. Nothing, however, indicates that he is exempting some same-sex intercourse as acceptable. It is all an abomination for Paul. The mutuality implied in his description of what is attacked "for one another",[297] makes it unlikely that he is addressing only one-sided exploitative relations, as in pederasty. He employs the language of shame and dishonour,[298] though never explicitly referring to males being shamed by becoming females. Indeed, his declaration of perversion applies to both men and women and to both the active and the passive partners. The allusion literally to

---

[292] *T. Levi* 14:6; *T. Naph.* 4:1; *T. Benj.* 9:1.

[293] *T. Levi* 17:11.

[294] Rom 1:24-28.

[295] Rom 1:20-25, 28; Wis 14:12.

[296] Rom 1:24, 26, 27.

[297] Rom 1:27.

[298] Rom 1:24, 26, 27.

"males" and "females"[299] probably has in mind, the creation of male and female,[300] which along with the prohibitions of Leviticus[301] will have shaped Paul's stance. It is interesting that the argument about procreation and so perversion of intercourse from its purpose of propagation does not appear in his statements, but that is also consistent with Paul's comments about sexuality elsewhere.

In 1 Corinthians Paul employs a list of people who are disqualified from entering God's kingdom, among whom are some, called in Greek *arsenokoitai* ("bedding males") and *malakoi* ("soft").[302] The former occurs also in the first letter to Timothy composed in Paul's name.[303] The terms are best understood as references to people engaged in same-sex intercourse, in their active and passive roles, the latter word used also more widely in disapproval of the effeminate. Paul's use of the word may indicate that he shared the view of the shamefulness of men acting as women, despite not saying so directly in Romans, but the evidence is too slim to be sure, occurring as it does in a list without further commentary.

The only other probable reference to same-sex relations is limited to pederasty, where it makes best sense of the severe warning issued by Jesus against causing little ones to stumble, a common metaphor for sexual failing.[304] In this case the issue is abuse of children and, while not explicitly mentioning sexual abuse, most likely has it in mind. The following context, which challenges people to cut off hands and feet and pluck out eyes,[305] may also have been addressing sexual wrongdoing originally, not least because Matthew uses such sayings explicitly to warn against sexual sin.[306] Much less certain is the proposal that in bringing children to Jesus for him to "touch" (another word used also in sexual contexts), people had sexual engagement in mind, such as is alleged of some teachers of the day, who would exploit especially prepubescent youth, and could explain the strength of the disciples' response.[307] It is difficult, however, to imagine this occurring in first century Galilee, though it is possible that the story might have been heard in this way by some in other contexts. Apart from these, nothing suggests that the centurion must have had a sexual relation with his slave,[308] as

---

[299] Rom 1:26, 27.

[300] Gen 1:27.

[301] Lev 18:22; 20:13.

[302] 1 Cor 6:9-10.

[303] 1 Tim 1:9-10.

[304] Mark 9:42.

[305] Mark 10:43-48.

[306] Matt 5:29-30.

[307] Mark 10:13-16.

[308] Cf. Matt 8:5-13; Luke 7:1-10; cf. John 4:46-53.

some speculate, nor that the reference to eunuchs really means people born with homosexual orientation.[309]

Paul shared with his contemporaries the view that human beings were either male or female. He would have agreed with Philo (and, it seems Plato, himself) in laughing off Aristophanes' myth which claimed that some people are naturally inclined towards members of their own sex. While in Paul's world that idea comes to the surface occasionally, though rarely, we can be fairly confident that Paul and his fellow Jews would have rejected the notion. For Paul, failure to respond rightly to God led to people failing to live rightly and so allowing their passions to take over and produce in them behaviour which was both unnatural and a transgression of divine order and command. Paul sees no need to argue for this view, but rather believes he can assume it as undisputed among his hearers and therefore can use it as a basis for what he does go on to argue, namely that all others are sinful, too.[310]

Though his brief exposition is incidental to his larger purpose, Paul's analysis has its own logic. Perversion in one area leads to perversion in the other. In both it is sin. To be so overcome by your sexual feelings that you act contrary to what is natural for you, resulting in acts which contradict who you are is depravity and perversion in his view. Of course, for people who find themselves naturally oriented towards their own kind, such a judgement necessarily falls wide of the mark, but we should not blame Paul for that. He wrote according to his understanding. Nor then does it make sense to blame people who are not engaged in perversion but who are simply following their orientation with as much control and maturity as those otherwise oriented. Nothing, however, indicates that Paul entertained such a possibility.

What emerges from this review of what writers said about sexual passions is that wherever belief in creation informs their attitudes, sex and sexual passion is seen as something positive. Even where, as in the case especially of Philo and the *Testaments of the Twelve Patriarchs*, there is strong influence trending in the direction of condemning sexual passion as evil, the writers stop short of doing so, but instead advise strict control. Even the dominant focus on the role of sexual intercourse for propagation of the species mostly does not expunge the sense that sexual intercourse entails pleasure, which is hedged about with provisions which confine it to marriage. Anything outside of that context is out of order and so condemned as sin, which thus encompasses a wide range of activities. For some, sin includes sex within marriage where procreation is not the focus. For most, the dual focus reflected in the creation stories of propagation and companionship allows legitimacy where either of the latter is the goal, though in their day, unlike ours with effective contraception, such distinctions were mostly irrelevant, though

---

[309] Matt 19:12.

[310] Rom 3:9, 23; 1:16 – 3:26.

not entirely. Increasingly the focus was not just on actions but attitudes, which resulted in attention to sexual passion and its direction, especially where intense, and here assumptions about what was natural, as God's creation intended it, determined that what was deemed unnatural such as both passion and action towards members of one's own sex was abhorrent. The seriousness with which philosophers of the day, whose influence shaped the views of the writings we have considered, addressed matters of sexual desire and behaviour, deserves respect as belonging to some of the most profound discussions of the human condition ever produced. Attitudes to sexual passion and sexual behaviour inherent in these texts have significantly shaped ethical thought to our own day and so warrant respectful critical engagement in our very different world.

Conclusion

As noted in the Introduction, the overview presented in the four chapters of this book is a distillation of the findings of five volumes of research, encompassing over 2400 pages of detailed discussion. That research was undertaken as an attempt to listen as closely as possible to what various writers were saying in their world and in their terms about sexuality. Engaging ancient texts requires the discipline of careful method but also the acknowledgement that as scholars we have limitations, may miss some detail or see it in a distorted way because of our own perspective or experience. Hence the importance of engaging not only the texts, but also the community of scholarship already engaged with these texts.

This book does not take the reader into detailed discussions of either the texts or the scholarship concerning them, but presupposes them and so directs the reader to those detailed treatments for further information. As an aid to further exploration it appends a Subject Index which covers not just this book but all five volumes which were part of the detailed research. Through it readers will be able to pursue the subject matter in detail.

The purpose of this concluding chapter is to reflect on the sense of distance and proximity which consideration of this material evokes. To engage this material is truly to engage in a cross-cultural encounter across two thousand years. Even then it is not a matter of engaging one particular writing in one place at one particular time, but a range of literature written over four centuries in different places, in Hebrew, Aramaic, and Greek, and sometimes accessible only in another language like Latin or Ethiopic. What they have in common is a Jewish cultural heritage, but even then this is far from monochrome and reflects diverse influences, not least from surrounding cultures, and in our period from the pervasive Greco-Roman world of fashions and ideas.

Distance

Let me begin with the sense of distance. We are looking back to a time when people thought the world was flat or something like it. Most believed it was populated by demons, and many, that its history would soon be brought to an end by divine intervention. Their notions of cosmogony, how the universe came into being, what produces sickness and disease, indeed how the human reproductive system works, were vastly different from our own. The same is true across a whole range of other matters of knowledge and understanding.

One might opt to be dismissive or one can acknowledge such differences not in a patronising manner but with respect, while at the same time not compromising one's integrity. Engagement with respect entails being able to disagree when necessary, allowing others to be wrong where we are convinced they are wrong and not being crippled by a sense that somehow what we see as truth cannot be applied to such texts, just as in future some may well have to say the same about us with similar respect.

With regard to matters broadly related to sexuality we also sense distance. In most, though not all, societies today but probably the ones where most of us as readers are at home, marriages are not arranged by parents, but are formed solely on the basis of choice between two partners. Mostly they form the basis of so-called nuclear families within communities where there is health care, aged care, and facilities for support, such as education, hospitals and the like. This is in stark contrast to the ancient household, which if not self-sufficient, was at least tied to systems of dependence on more wealthy patrons and closely connected with extended families whose concerns were dominant.

Ages at marriage in our societies are quite different and variable, compared to theirs of men being mostly around thirty and women in their teens. Common assumptions in our day do not rate women as inferior, though we are still in many respects not as far along that journey as we could be. Creation stories read as depicting a hierarchy with men above women no longer convince. Assumptions that women have less emotional control than men would not find general acceptance today as they did then. We assume women are equal to men also in leadership and in many, though not all, churches this is reflected in the ordination of both men and women to ministry. Most today would see parenting roles as something to be shared equally even if differently between men and women and would not want to perpetuate what first century writers saw as the most respectable and divinely authorised order of women obeying husbands.

The promise to obey has thus disappeared from the promises of most wedding vows, replaced by promises including mutual respect. While the ritual of giving the bride away traces its origins to the notion of a father handing his daughter into the authority of another male, her husband, most have either dispensed with the practice or at least observe it in a manner that is no longer intended to imply subordination. Similarly the values which led Paul to instruct that women remain silent in church unless they have exceptional callings and that they continue to be veiled when they enter communities of worship, no longer carry weight for most today, though one may find them in contemporary cross-cultural encounter.

As we have seen, some of the assumptions about women's inferiority would have been perpetuated by the fact that men usually married wives little more than half their age and so less knowledgeable, less experienced, and so at least in those senses inferior. Most of our marriages assume equal partnership and certainly not inequalities in one direction in relation to knowledge and experience.

We are also no longer faced with one of the reasons why fathers felt they should marry off their daughters while young, namely fear of pregnancy. One may dispute the assumption that young women were less able to control themselves than young men, but for us the major change is much more recent and has been with us for barely half a century, namely effective and safe methods of contraception. That has not only made it possible for more women to enter the workforce and for couples to plan their families. It has also removed one of the main rationales for many of the sexual prohibitions, so much so that where people continue to uphold them they have needed to redefine their rationales.

The impact of the advent of contraception is to be seen in the acceptance with which most approach the widespread social pattern of people living together while not married, whether as people who have not yet married or people who have been divorced or widowed and have not entered new marriages. It has also caused people to rethink the ideal of virginity, which back then and for most of history was seen as a guarantee that a woman might remain chaste during marriage and was deemed as the appropriate state in which to enter marriage. With the fear of pregnancy removed which strongly governed such concerns, people have had to reassess the weight given to pre-marital chastity, thus focusing on values such as the need to give attention to boundaries and vulnerabilities in the formation of intimate relations. By and large what we see as teenage dating and romance would have been rendered impossible by the controls of the ancient family, so that issues of managing it and setting its boundaries, especially in view of contraception, have been a new challenge.

For the same reason and perhaps with more solid grounds people have had to revisit matters like adultery, which despite the removal of the threat of pregnancy most partners find intolerable for other reasons which seem as alive now as they were then, such as unwillingness to share sexual intimacy with more than one partner. Again the rationales for dealing with matters such as multipartnering and prostitution have had to be informed by such changes. Arguments that wasted semen, whether within or beyond marriage or in masturbation, creates a potential crisis for the survival of the species because semen may run out and virility diminish meet our smile, not our assent.

For most today the formal practice of polygyny is out of the question as is the assumption that the male head of the house should have sexual rights over all females in his household beyond those forbidden by the laws of incest. We recognise the sexual abuse implied in this but also in much else that was acceptable then, including their rules enshrined in biblical law about dealing with rape and about captive women. Our laws of incest differ from those of ancient times. Most notably what John the Baptist (and presumably Jesus) objected to about Herod Antipas's marrying his stepbrother's divorced wife would be considered legal in most jurisdictions today, as would marrying one's stepmother once widowed, a prospect which offended Paul at Corinth.

The practice of celibacy of priests does not derive from the literature which we have considered, but arose at a much later date. The forms of celibacy which did exist were mainly temporary, not permanent, and related to special places and special times. Nevertheless some of the presuppositions which generated the practice are to be found back then. They include those notions of sacred space and time, which were present in many cultures, and the belief that the age to come would be fully a sacred space and time and so sexual engagement would cease, the belief that sexual passions are to be suppressed, and the pragmatics of believing that unmarried people would have more time and energy at their disposal than the married. While the practice has clearly worked for most, there have been too many for whom it has not and who have sought to give expression to their natural sexual passions in ways that have been exploitative and abusive. One of the challenges faced by those who espouse lifelong celibacy of priests is whether the rationales for requiring it are still cogent, including whether they outweigh the dangers posed by its unnatural restrictions.

Another area where values have changed is divorce, which, while an accepted part of Jewish culture, came in some circles to be challenged in the light of apparently irresponsible use and even to be opposed, such as in the sayings and responses to the issue attributed to Jesus. Most, including most churches, though not all, no longer apply an absolute prohibition, but take an approach which calls for each situation to be assessed in its own right, which may result in partners resolving that divorce is the lesser of two evils and the way to new beginnings, including entering a new marriage. Others engage in the juggle of affirming the prohibition but seeking to find grounds for declaring the marriage invalid in the first place.

The assumption shared by those cultures was that adultery warranted, indeed required, divorce. Matthew's version of Jesus' prohibition articulates it as an exception to the prohibition of divorce, but it was probably the hidden assumption in the prohibition from the beginning. Adultery as at least ground for divorce, though not necessarily mandating it, belonged on the statute books of many societies well into the twentieth century. In most jurisdictions, where divorce is handled in courts today, no such rule applies. Secular wisdom has seen that the demise of a marriage is usually much more complex, and theological reflection has also supported the notion that there can be a place for reconciliation and healing, whether that is in termination or rebuilding the relationship, a thoroughly biblical perspective in a deeper sense.

Proximity

Already our discussion of handling divorce has alerted us to values which continue to shape modern attitudes across two thousand years. Such values tend to be found not in commands and prohibitions, but in attitudes and ideas. An underlying assumption of the writings we have considered is that the God of Israel and so the God of all is interested in restoration and healing. That comes to expression in notions of forgiveness and reconciliation or restored relationships, a strong feature also of the New Testament writings. This puts issues of divorce and remarriage and dealing with the complexities of relationship issues in a new or wider perspective, sufficient for many to see the possibilities of forgiveness and healing or new beginnings outweighing the absolutes of prohibiting divorce, and certainly of the mandating of divorce where adultery has taken place.

Another key value which, as we saw, prevented even those most influenced by contemporary denigration of passions, especially sexual passions, such as Philo, from outlawing sex, was the idea of divine creation. It meant that they could not allow themselves to declare sex or sexual desire evil. That affirmation of sex continues to inform contemporary perspectives of our own day. It has not always been easy to sustain because some texts have been wrongly read as implying that sexual response is something about which to feel guilty. References to "flesh" have been misconstrued as anti-sex. People have also misread Jesus' statement about looking lustfully at another's wife with a view to wanting to have sex with her as a condemnation of all responses of men to all women and so as constituting adultery of the heart. More careful listening to the text itself and to the values embedded in the tradition have exposed the misreading. It is not about all women, which would imply women are a danger, but about the wives of others and not about sexual response but sexual intent. Thus rather than implicitly to blame women's sexuality and so require that they be feared and controlled, it addresses men, insisting they take responsibility for how they respond to their sexual feelings.

Closely associated with the valuing of sex as part of God's creation is the valuing of human beings, men and women. Here the engagement with the creation stories which have their origin in near eastern myth, has required a more subtle appreciation than for many centuries had been the case. While some might still insist on believing literally in creation as an event less than 10,000 years back that took place over 7 days, in which men were formed from earth and women from a man's rib, most people today acknowledge that the beginnings of this vast universe are much more complex, reaching back over millions of years of evolution, including of the human species in its gendered forms. To select some texts like the creation of humankind in God's image and as male and female as somehow exempt from the critical historical perspective which recognises myth, is an oddity, though such motifs have been a fruitful stimulus for reflection. Using the Genesis stories also for claiming male superiority, let alone women's susceptibility to uncontrolled passion, sits strangely with an approach which seeks to respect cross-cultural difference. Again, values which affirm male and female, alongside Jew and gentile and slave and free, such as we find asserted by Paul, have the potential to undermine and revise the assumptions with which he and authors of his time operated.

The revision of their assumptions about the inequality of men and women, and the rejection of their assumptions that slavery was acceptable and slaves inferior or to be kept in their place, has taken many centuries, but has become established in principle if not always in practice, in most contexts. Both a common sense of justice and an openness to biblical values helped people to make those important transitions.

The much more controversial issue about which many churches are divided, is over same-sex relations and whether people with a same-sex orientation, men or women, who express themselves in sexual intimacy with a person of their own sex, should have places of leadership in the church and community and whether their long term committed relationships should also be understood as marriages.

The findings of my research indicate that in all the literature which I examined the assumption is that such actions and the attitudes, passions, which produce them were abhorrent. Both the prohibition of Leviticus, which authors understood as condemning such acts (some extending this explicitly to such acts between women), and the creation story which reports that God made (only) male and female, underlie that stance. There is no evidence that any of the Jewish writers actually believed that there were people with a natural sexual orientation towards people of their own sex. Philo, who mentions that view, declares it absurd. These writers, typified by Paul, believed then that people engaging such passions and doing such things were acting contrary to their nature and to be condemned. In fact, along with idolatry, same sex relations were a major target in Jewish criticism of the depravity of the world in which they lived.

Many still hold to this view, though some do so with the modification that they acknowledge that some people do seem to be naturally attracted to members of the same sex, i.e. are homosexual, a belief in which they differ from our writers. They have reached this view, as most indicate, by observing contemporary experience. Those for whom for ideological reasons biblical prohibitions must remain intact then counsel that homosexuals are to be respected and understood but to be required not to express their sexual desires in same sex-relations. For others, including myself, this goes halfway in distancing from first century views and produces a cruel conclusion. Why can these people for whom a homosexual orientation is natural not express themselves sexually in the same responsible way we ask of heterosexual people? Informing the stance that calls for dropping such discrimination against homosexuals are values of natural justice but also of the same biblical principles which have revised other forms of discrimination. The fact that in relation to slaves and women one can find hints of a better approach in these writings, but not in relation to homosexuals, is no reason not to follow the path of non discrimination.

Coming Together

Engagement with another human being entails respecting distance and being open to proximity. I need to acknowledge that I cannot fully know another. I must resist the temptation to short-cut my encounter by selective hearing and reading into what people say only what I want to hear. Respecting the otherness, indeed, the holiness of another human being means trying to hear them in their terms, in their context, in their language. It means being open to who they are, whether that is pleasant or not, whether I like what they say or not. My relating is not authentic if I hear only the good things and idealise the other. In fact, on the receiving end to be treated like that is threatening, quite apart from usually being not true. Nor is my relating authentic if I hear only the negative and demonise the other. If I take my encounter with another seriously, I need to take responsibility for my responses. This is true at a sexual level. I need to respect distance and boundaries. It is true of individual relationships in general. It is certainly true of encountering ancient texts, such as those with which this research has been engaged.

Many, though not all, of them are revered texts. Usually we engage such texts because our community or our own experience has taught us that they inspire, they can jump the gap between now and then and address us. They still deserve to be treated with respect, in fact all the more so because of the role we give them. That means embracing the discipline of careful and informed listening and avoiding jumping to conclusions because they are so familiar we think we know what they mean and have perhaps become accustomed to read them with little regard or sensitivity to their context. They deserve better than this. To hail their authority as a basis for not doing so is foolish and ultimately irresponsible and disrespectful. The investigations summarised in this book are intended to enhance respectful and careful reading.

Other texts carry no special weight and meet us as strangers across time, sometimes surprising us with unfamiliar insights, sometimes confronting us with the bizarre. Among the latter are those which make much of the myth of the angels, the Watchers, who had sexual relations with women, who gave birth to giants, from whose corpses evils spirits then emerged. Not surprisingly this had much more credibility in those times than it has in ours and explains the focus on exorcisms and the cry for God's reign to banish such forces. But even this myth has its truth to tell, especially if we understand that it was trying to account for the human condition. What they personalised as demons, many related to illness and disease, we might describe as viruses and the like. The myth gave expression to human vulnerability both at the level of illness and disease and at the level of political oppression. Our namings are different but their aspirations remain key aspirations in our own day. Interestingly what began as an account of gross sexual misdemeanour quickly leaves the sexual aside and focuses on larger issues. One might well reflect that today, too, there are much bigger issues that need our attention than the sexual misdemeanours, important as they may be.

As we saw, the book of *Jubilees* reworks the story in Genesis 2 to highlight sexual intimacy as one of God's chief aims for the first man and woman. The goal of human reproduction was important, but that was not everything or even essential and would wait till they had spent their time in the garden and then been expelled. The goal of sexual union belonged to God's goal of human companionship before they entered the garden and, while in *Jubilees* it was modelled first by the animals, it became the foundation of human community and a profound expression of love. That is where it belongs and what makes it not only right but good.

Ultimately the most important text pertaining to sexuality in the writings we have considered is the commandment to love one's neighbour as oneself. And the most important sexual organ is not this or that aspect of our genitalia, but our brain. This book has been an invitation to engage what was said two thousand years ago with a view to enabling more informed choices and perspectives on what it means to be a responsible sexual being today.

Index of Ancient Sources

References in brackets immediately under the title of a work indicate where extension discussion of that work may be found in volumes 1 – 5 of *Attitudes towards Sexuality in Judaism and Christianity in the Hellenistic Greco-Roman Era.*

Index of Subjects

This index provides a selection of subjects dealt with both in all five volumes of the research upon which this book is based and in this book itself. The five volumes are:

1. *Enoch, Levi, and Jubilees on Sexuality: Attitudes towards Sexuality in the Early Enoch Literature, the Aramaic Levi Document, and the Book of Jubilees* (Grand Rapids: Eerdmans, 2007)
2. *The Dead Sea Scrolls on Sexuality: Attitudes towards Sexuality in Sectarian and Related Literature at Qumran* (Grand Rapids: Eerdmans, 2009)
3. *The Pseudepigrapha on Sexuality: Attitudes towards Sexuality in Apocalypses, Testament, Legends, Wisdom, and Related Literature* (Grand Rapids: Eerdmans, 2011)
4. *Philo, Josephus, and the Testaments on Sexuality: Attitudes towards Sexuality in the Writings of Philo, Josephus, and the Testaments of the Twelve Patriarchs* (Grand Rapids: Eerdmans, 2011)
5. *The New Testament on Sexuality* (Grand Rapids: Eerdmans, 2012)

The first entry reference in this index is to this book, followed by references to the volumes above; thus **3**.336 refers to volume **3** page 336. Numbers in italics indicate thematic summaries of the subject. Volume **5** also contains summaries which incorporate findings from volumes **1-4**.

Abortion 61; **3**.466-67, 508; **4**.244, 355; **5**.82

Abraham and Hagar 49, 117; **1**.292, 295; **4**.153-55

Abraham and Sarah 49, 59, 68-69, 83, 86; **1**.150-152, 250-56; **2**.294-97; **3**.485-86; **4**.149-56, 271-73, 275-76, 394; **5**.7-8, 21-22

Adam and Eve 47, 95-96; **1**.286; **2**.229-30; **3**.27-28, 41-44, 68-74, 85-93, 101-102, 108-109, 498-501; **4**.15-16, 110-17

Adultery 33-34, 47, 63-74, 110, 113, 115; **1**.36, 169, 178, 200-203, 294; **2**.36-37, 111, 116-17, 123; **3**.56-68, 134-35, 493-94, 503-504; **4**.188-93, 283, 308, 314-15, 317, 321-23, 332-33, 349-50; **5**.4-9, 76-77, 109-38

Adultery: allegation 65, 140; **2**.153-56, 352; **4**.185 224-25, 321

Adultery: attitude 67-68, 140; **5**.109-19, 139-42

Adultery: mandating divorce 68-70; **1**.151, 198, 295; **2**.294-96; **3**.49, 486; **4**.155, 201, 272-73, 381; **5**.6-9, 76 77, 103-104, 249, 491-92

Adultery: sex with a betrothed woman 65; **4**.227-28; **5**.9-10, 139

Alcohol 16, 24, 57, 111. 119, 134; **1**.146-47, 197; **2**.306, **3**.62, 107, 143, 146, 203, 205, 237, 372, 386, 389, 425, 497-98, 505; **4**.67, 78-79, 98, 124, 129, 141, 145-46, 157-58, 163, 202, 209, 217, 223, 234-36, 255, 271, 275, 279, 293, 303, 317, 328, 373, 381-82, 390, 401-10, 413, 421-22, 430, 435; **5**.21, 30, 33, 47, 231-32, 235, 238-39, 293, 306, 324-26, 348

Alexander Janneus 5, 36, 66; **4**.304

Anal intercourse 121-23, 133, 136; **3**.46, 53, 110, 137, 469, 508; **5**.310, 316

Anna 72, 115; **3**.209; **5**.447

Antipas 41, 62, 72, 130; **4**.318; **5**.143-46. 273

Antony and Cleopatra 135; **4**.306-309

Aristobulus, brother of Mariamme 135; **4**.306

Aristophanes 11, 21, 107, 134, 139; **4**.16, 26, 211, 216; **5**.33

161